C000200956

PROPERTY OF BARNSLEY SoBS GROUP
IF FOUND PLEASE EMAIL
barnsley@uksobs.org

Do They Have Bad Days in Heaven?

Surviving the Suicide Loss of a Sibling

By Michelle Linn-Gust (Rusk), Ph.D.

CHELLEHEAD
WORKS

Do They Have Bad Days in Heaven? Surviving the Suicide Loss of a Sibling, Third Edition

Copyright © 2020 by Michelle L. Rusk

ISBN: 978-0-9837776-8-7

Library of Congress Control Number: 2020912893

info@chelleheadworks.com

505-266-3134

Albuquerque, New Mexico

Printed in the United States of America

First Edition printing, July 2001

Third Edition, First Printing September 2020

Redesign for third edition by Megan Mickey

Cover Photo by Marianne Linn, December 1975

In Memory of Denise Susanne Linn

1975-1993

—————————

*You always told me that if the palm tree
started dropping coconuts on my head to look to the other side.*

I wish you could have done the same.

—————————

Contents

Do They Have Bad Days in Heaven?

Acknowledgments

I didn't write this book in a vacuum nor have I have traveled on my grief road alone. And yet I don't think I could remember every name that belongs on this page because there are so many. And so many that came after the first edition of the book was published. I am grateful to all the people I met and shared conversations with, sometimes just a few minutes in a short space of time, because in some way you're all reflected here and in all my writing and creative endeavors.

Thank you also to my husband Greg who came into my life as I was forging a new path, for being supportive of me doing this edition, and for just letting me be me.

To my sister Karen for the laughter over our texts about nothing that have helped us both continue to forge forward after the losses of our parents and our sister.

To LaRita Archibald, John McIntosh, Rick Mogil, and Stephanie Weber enthusiastically helping me with this new edition. And to Megan Mickey for not being daunted by opening a 19-year-old Quark file.

Do They Have Bad Days in Heaven?

Foreword

During the summer of 1993 while interning at the Olympic Training Center in Colorado Springs Michelle Linn attended HEARTBEAT, the suicide survivor support group I founded and facilitated. Michelle's 17-year-old sister, Denise, had ended her life several months before by stepping in front of a train. Michelle was still reeling from the horror and manner of Denise's death. A petite blond, Michelle looked more like a frail, terrified child stranded without friend or family than the college journalism junior she claimed to be. As I drove her back to the OTC that night she spoke of her struggle to focus on her internship, of feeling disconnected from her family, from reality. She questioned whether she played a role in Denise's act, even her own sanity and ability to move forward into the future. I listened with intense interest and concern. I had four children who survived their brother's suicide and was compelled to understand the perspective of a sibling survivor.

After my 24-year-old son killed himself, those expressing sympathy usually directed their words of comfort to his father and myself, bypassing his three brothers and sister as if their sorrow and loss was minimal. My daughter sobbed as she shared, "They told me to take care of you and Daddy…I'm so sorry, Mom, but I can't even take care of me." My oldest son was attending graduate school in the Midwest. I assumed he was busy and better without my frequent calls inquiring of his well-being. Wrong! He called one day to tell me. "Don't forget about me. I feel so alone and I am so sad." He expressed a deep sense of responsibility for not having been available when his brother needed him. The next youngest brother was the only one of our children at home the night his brother shot himself so he shouldered an immense burden of horror, police, hospital and being "in charge." The youngest brother, fourteen and just entering the high school all siblings had attended, was subjected to remarks about himself, his brother and our family by both students and staff (Remember! This was in 1978 when the issue of suicide was still very much taboo).

Each of my four surviving children was reluctant to share their feelings with me not wishing to add their pain to my own. Although we grieved the loss of the same person, we each grieved the loss of a different relationship. I knew the grief of losing a child but had no insight into the grief of losing a brother or sister. I felt great sorrow for this traumatic interruption in their young lives, such fear for their futures. I so badly wanted some understanding of their grief needs and how those needs could best be met. My search for materials addressing sibling grief resulted in brief mention in books on the subject and absolutely nothing when the cause of death was suicide.

Then came Michelle! That night in 1993 was the beginning of a lifelong friendship despite our three decade age difference. She grew interested in the study of suicide as a preventable health issue, became deeply involved in the American Association of Suicidology and was eventually elected president. We were roommates at these conferences for numerous years. We presented at one another's workshops and visited one another's homes. I listened and absorbed what Michelle shared about her grief journey, specifically as a surviving sister. She referred to grieving siblings as the forgotten mourners which related to my daughter's comments. The more I learned from Michelle the more I urged her to put what she had experienced into a book. Finally, *Do They Have Bad Days in Heaven?* was published, among the first accounts of grief after the suicide of a sibling. This book normalizes the feelings of those losing a sibling to suicide and offers suggestions for healing the terrible wounds associated with the loss. It is a book of love, of family, of pain and most importantly, a book of hope. From sibling suicide bereaved and their concerned families everywhere… Thank you, Michelle, for your gift of sharing your loss and unchartered steps toward healing. The growth, success and dreams you've achieved since writing *Do They Have Bad Days in Heaven?* reminds all survivors that we have a life beyond the suicide of our loved one…wholeness to regain, dreams to follow, and happiness to enjoy.

The New Edition, 2020

I will be honest, I didn't want to do a new edition of this book.

For five years, I had poured myself into writing it and I can still remember sitting on the stoop of the back door of the house where I was living– just five down from where I live now– and thumbing through the book after the boxes had arrived. It was hard to believe it was finally real.

I had no idea what was ahead, but I also remember just months before, saying goodbye to my then-husband at the airport when I was going to my first American Association of Suicidology conference, order forms for the not-quite-published book that had just been copied in my bag. I knew then that my life wasn't going to be the same when I returned home.

And it wasn't. The last nineteen years have been quite an adventure to say the least. As I get ready to delve into the changes I need to make for the new edition, I know that none of the story will change. Mostly, I will update any statistics and information and the language we use around suicide, all that have changed. The internet as we know it today, was vastly different and limited when this book was first published so the resources will change as well.

I wrote *Bad Days* (as I call it) because there wasn't a way for sibling survivors of suicide to connect. It was nearly eighteen months after my sister died that I met fellow sibling survivor outside my family (I have two surviving siblings and I also don't often mention that my maternal grandmother had lost her brother to suicide in the ten years before I was born).

After *Bad Days* was published in July 2001 and the fear of 9-11 wore off– leaving me with book signings where no one showed up; you could see the look of fear as people walked by the table and saw the title of the book– I began to speak not just in the United States, but around the world. My work in New Mexico thrived as the state was ready to tackle the issue. I traveled between dusty local roads on the pueblos and the Navajo Nation to as far as beaches in the South Pacific off Australia's eastern coast to give talks on not just sibling suicide grief, but suicide grief and suicide prevention.

It led to a doctorate in family studies, a number of new books on suicide grief, and the presidency of the American Association of Suicidology.

And then I felt as if I had done what I needed to do.

I'd been telling my story and Denise's story and I had enjoyed every minute of it. I knew I was lucky to have so much support and opportunity because of it. And I knew that Denise was proud of me.

But I also had the sense that if she could talk to me, she would have said, "I appreciate all you've done for siblings, but don't forget the writer you wanted to be before I died."

I was twenty-one when she died, and well into my thirties when my suicide work took off. I didn't want to wake up at sixty or seventy and wish I had done other things. I hadn't had the opportunity to truly explore life without suicide in it all the time.

My first husband suffered a head injury when he was hit by a drunk driver in 2003 and our marriage was dissolved in 2011. My dad died in 2006 (my mom in 2014). For me, the deaths of my parents felt much closer to me than Denise's death because so much life had happened between her death in 1993 and my dad's death in 2006. It was like I was gathering family members in heaven.

I returned to my fiction and published several books, I ran a divorced women's group at my church because I still felt I had something to offer. I worked on several military grief projects. And I launched Chelle Summer.

My lifestyle brand Chelle Summer takes a different side of me, the creative one that had put sewing away for a number of years and allowed me to use the memories of the Barbie clothes Denise and I played with, the colorful prints and patterns of the seventies, and make them something else in my adult life.

I started with bucket bags, using vintage fabrics whenever possible, and ventured into clothes and swimsuits. And aprons. It was what I called retro design with a modern twist. It made me feel more connected to Denise and the childhood that only I get to share with the world because she isn't here with me. And it connected me with Mom who was fearless with color and prints although I didn't realize it until I was an adult.

During this time though, the boxes of *Bad Days* from the fifth printing began to dwindle. I knew the day was coming and I would have to make a decision about what to do about the book. There would be no printing thousands of books this time with the ease of on-demand printing and ebooks. But could we get a 19-year-old Quark file open into something so I didn't have to retype the book?

I was ready to give up and move on, to send it out of print. After all, there have been many books published since mine and the social media and the internet make it easier for people to connect.

But as I write this, the pandemic and the division in not just the United States, but around the world, continue to fester. Suicides have been increasing in the years since I moved into doing other things, yet I have grave concerns that they will continue to rise as everything drags out.

My designer Megan Mickey magically opened the file and here we are. We have a new cover and there are updates, but I'm going to try and leave the story as I wrote it nineteen years ago. Some of it has changed as my perspective has changed (for instance, I don't believe there are bad days in heaven now, but that was just one of the questions I asked after Denise died, one of the things I might not have ever questioned if she hadn't died). Still, it's important that that aspect of the story remain as it was in the original story.

What happened to Denise doesn't change. My reactions all those years ago don't change. That part of the story is the same and it still resonates with sibling survivors of suicide all these years later.

Do They Have Bad Days in Heaven?

Introduction, 2001

We specifically requested a plot under some trees to lay Denise's body to rest. One summer day, seven years later, my dad visited the cemetery and saw that a tree by Denise's grave had been cut down. "Diseased," they told my mom when she called. The spot we picked for Denise's body wasn't special anymore. It took more time to find her grave now because it wasn't obvious. My parents recently bought a new tree and had it planted in Denise's name, but it will take years to establish the same amount of shade that the old tree provided. Of everything that has changed since my sister died in 1993, the last place I expected to be different was the cemetery.

Almost a decade after her suicide, I still contemplate whether there are bad days in heaven. I never considered it until Denise died. True, she's finally out of her pain, but does she look down on us and feel sad when she sees how her death had affected our lives? There's no way she could have foreseen how her death would impact her family and friends. How could she, with all the anguish she was suffering? But after finding herself in heaven, is it as wonderful as they say or does she sigh, watching us scream and curse at her through our grief?

People tell me there can't possibly be bad days in the afterlife. Many have said it's because the Bible says so. Still, I cling to my doubts. Denise's death changed my life. And when our lives are reorganized, we must step back and reevaluate our beliefs. For me, nothing has been the same since March 18, 1993. I question everything about life more now because my sister's death took something away from me. It forced me to grow in ways I wasn't ready for. If Denise hadn't died, I never would have contemplated whether there are bad days in heaven. But that's not my reality.

As we continue to drive through this course we call life, it never remains status quo. I learned that lesson the hard way. However, to this day, as I think about Denise looking down on me, I still wonder, "Do they have bad days in heaven?"

Do They Have Bad Days in Heaven?

Chapter One

We're Never Going to See Her Again

My mom doesn't remember this, but early in my college career I asked her how someone goes on after the death of a loved one. For no particular reason, I had been thinking about the loss of a spouse and wondered how people dealt with losing someone so close to them. I was baffled at how one continued life after a death.

Little did I know I would have to find my own way through grief only a year after I made the comment. My younger sister Denise ended her life two weeks before her eighteenth birthday, two months before her high school graduation. We would become "The Tuesday Night Movie" that no one ever believes can happen to them.

When I talk about my sister's death, I'm never sure where to begin. Do I start from when we were children and I put tape across the rug of our room to keep her off my side? Do I start with her falling grades following two perfect high school semesters? Or do I begin with her first suicide attempt the October before she died? What about the night before her death when I came home from college unexpectedly? There are so many parts to this story.

In the spring of 1993, as a junior majoring in journalism at Ball State University in Muncie, Indiana, I covered the men's basketball team for *The Ball State Daily News*. The season was a whirlwind and before I knew it, the team had won the Mid-American Conference Tournament in March. The next step was the NCAA Tournament. I was excited watching the seeding show (deciding where the Cardinals would play in the tournament) on television, figuring I would be traveling out west, either to Utah or Arizona to cover the team. But when Ball State's seed appeared on the black-and-white television in the newsroom, I saw I would be going home to Chicago instead. Disappointed that I was not headed to a warmer climate for a few days, I spent the night before the game at my parents' house in the suburbs. It was my first trip home since the Christmas break.

Although it was nice to go home, it also meant I had to be reminded of Denise's recent difficulties, which seemed very far away while I was at school. She had swallowed 250 aspirin the previous fall, but told Mom the next morning that she didn't want to die. It was then that we learned of her hidden bulimia and just how severe her depression had become. After she spent a week in the eating disorders unit of a psychiatric hospital, all seemed well when I returned home for Thanksgiving. She also had a boyfriend whom she really liked.

At Christmas, everything was fine except the one night she returned home from spending time with friends and got angry at me for "turning everything into a joke," even though to this day, I don't remember what I said that made her so mad. My older sister Karen went into Denise's room to comfort her. Mom and I stood by the banister in the hallway. Mom shook her head; she wasn't sure what to do anymore. What would make Denise happy?

I only talked to Denise twice between January and when I went home for the basketball game in March. One of those times, she had called and left a message on my answering machine saying she just wanted to talk. I didn't call her back because I had just returned from a road trip to Central Michigan University and had two basketball stories to write. There always will be times for us to talk, I thought.

She was the youngest in our family and the closest to me in age. We were three-and-a-half years apart. Eleven years separated her and Brian, the oldest. Karen is a year younger than Brian. We are supposed to grow old with our siblings.

Denise and I grew up sharing a room for ten years. We were childhood playmates. We made up games, roller skated together in the basement, and drew pictures that we "sold" to family members. In the last few years of her life, we weren't as close because I was away at college, but she wrote me letters regularly. During one stressful time, she drew me a picture of a palm tree with a girl standing underneath that said, "When life drops a coconut on your head, don't forget to look to the other side of the palm tree."

On this St. Patrick's Day night in March, Denise was in good spirits. Karen was also home so the three Linn sisters could be together. We sat on Mom's bed and talked about Denise's plans to attend the University of Illinois at Chicago the next fall. Denise touched my hair and mentioned how I used to call my hair "golden locks." I had completely forgotten about that. Denise always remembered details I never could.

Ironically, earlier that day I visited my maternal grandmother who had broken her hip. Seeing her in a wheelchair at the nursing home brought tears to my eyes. She looked helpless, but still so happy to see me. Little did I know that sadness was nothing compared to what I was to experience only a day later.

The next morning, I knocked on Denise's door to see if she was going to get up for school. She mumbled something, and I left for my run. When I returned she was gone. While I read the newspaper over breakfast, the phone rang. It was the dean of students at her high school. My sister had ditched classes the day before to be with her friends on senior ditch day (a day in the spring when the seniors traditionally skip school) at the Catholic high school. My parents were furious, and Mom told the dean that my sister had to endure the punishment, a Saturday detention. I left for the basketball game, thankful I wasn't going to be there when she got home from school. When I met Jeff, the photographer I traveled with from Ball State, and shared Denise's behavior with him, he shrugged it off. He didn't understand that this wasn't like my sister.

But Denise never had to serve her Saturday detention. She walked out of the school shortly after that. Her counselor, aware of Denise's past suicide attempt, stopped her in the hall to ask if she was okay. Denise assured she was fine.

Somewhere along the line, Denise had decided she was going to die and this looked to be the perfect time. My sisters had planned to visit me a few weeks after the basketball season ended, but my trip home was a surprise. We believe it moved up her "dying date" because she had the opportunity to see me one last time.

She walked out of school, across the faculty parking lot, through the playing fields, and then past the industrial park that lined the railroad tracks. When a freight train approached, she stepped onto the tracks and held up her hands as if to say "I surrender." The train hit her at forty-nine miles per hour.

As the day wore on, my parents didn't become suspicious of anything until Denise's psychologist, a woman she respected, called to find out why Denise had missed her appointment. My sister really liked this woman and my parents didn't know why she chose not to go. They convinced themselves that she was at a friend's house, scared to come home because of the trouble she was in. Also, it was hard to understand why she chose to ditch school in the first place when Mom would have called her in sick for the day if she had asked.

The next morning, Mom and Dad alerted the Naperville police. They came by and asked what Denise had been wearing as my sister wore no identification, having left it in a coat still hanging in her locker. The police informed them of a pedestrian vs. train accident from the day before. Through her clothes and the fingerprints Mom had done when we were younger, Denise was positively identified.

In the meantime, I had returned to school following the game and set to writing my story, unaware that Denise was dead. On the way back to Muncie in the dark, it occurred to me that my sister might choose to die by suicide one day, but I didn't believe it would be then. I thought, maybe in a couple of years when I would have someone in my life to help me through my grief. I don't know why I thought so selfishly. Why did I think that in the first place anyway? Was it because she already had attempted suicide once? Oddly enough, when I had these disturbing thoughts, she was already dead.

Back at Ball State on Friday morning, I was glad the basketball season was over. My March 18, 1993, journal entry says:

We lost by twenty-two points, but at least it was a much better day (except Denise ditched school Wednesday morning and Mom and Dad found out while I was there...)...I'm glad (the basketball season) is over though. I can catch up on the rest of my life. Eight articles this week!

I set off to my Western Civilization class that morning after spending some time in *The Daily News* office. I don't remember my professor's name or much about that class. It was a requirement I had put off, and I got so far behind in the reading that I stopped opening the book at all. During the lecture that Friday, the pastor of my church in Muncie appeared at the door. I knew he was there for me. It was a big class and my professor called, "Is Michelle Linn here?" I followed Father John out into the hall. He looked upset.

"There's been an accident," he said.

"It's my sister, isn't it?" I knew. I don't remember many details after that. I gathered my things from the classroom, and we walked my bicycle to the church. I do recall telling him something about how I hadn't been to church much lately and had wondered if some bad things might happen because of it. He didn't say much, listening to me in my numbness.

When Father John and I arrived at St. Francis, Sister Rita was there and we called Mom. I asked Sister Rita to make the call. I knew Denise had radically changed our lives with her death and I feared confronting that. Sister Rita talked to Mom a few minutes before handing me the phone.

"We'll never see her again," Mom said, crying.

It was arranged that Sister Rita would drive me to Naperville. At my apartment, I had no idea what to pack. What was I going to wear to my sister's funeral? I grabbed textbooks, believing I would actually study.

I couldn't talk on the ride to Chicago. More than anything, I was scared of facing my family, knowing things had changed in a way we couldn't fix. Sister Rita tried to keep up the conversation for both of us. It was raining when we got into the Chicago area, cloudy and dreary. We drove to my parents' house where I dreaded facing the other side of the front door. Nothing would ever be the same again.

Strangely, there was an air of comfort in my parents' home. Everyone was there: my aunts (Mom's sisters Virginia and Janice), cousins, and others. Many people had come and gone while I was en route, too. I hugged Karen and my parents. We went into the kitchen and ate the meats and cheeses someone had brought for sandwiches. Sister Rita joked with my family, fitting right in with my family's Catholic ties. Talk turned to other subjects such as the basketball game I had just covered and the trip Karen and I had made to Nashville, Tennessee, only weeks before.

Soon, the crowd was gone, and only four of us were left: Mom, Dad, Karen, and me. I don't remember where Brian was. Dad called the funeral director so he could come over and start making plans for the burial.

We stayed up most of the night, talking and remembering Denise. We sat on the stairs in the dark and wondered: Should we have known? Had she given us any hints that we missed? Why did she decide to step in front of a train? Was school a problem? Had her bulimia returned? Did she ever have any sexual experiences? We would later find out she had been raped by a boy with whom she was acquainted. We knew his name was George, but that was it. The night during Christmas break she had run into her room because he forced himself on her a few hours earlier. She only told select friends and Karen. She said she would tell Mom after she worked it out with her psychologist, but that never happened.

I wrote in my journal that night, March 19, 1993:

It perplexes me, Denise standing in front of a train. I feel so upside down, but I'm constantly cracking jokes...I miss Denise. I want to wake up and have everything be okay. I can't believe she's gone. She had so much ahead of her. And I wish I had told her how cool she was more often.

Then there was the note. Mom told me they had searched a mile looking for a note the day my sister died. Someone in the industrial park had witnessed her reading something as she walked to the tracks, but no note was found. The morning after she died, one of Denise's friends found the suicide note in a box in Denise's room with notes she had collected from her friends.

The note must have provided some comfort for us at the time because my journal says I was relieved she died because she didn't love herself rather than because of something I did. The reality, however, was that it went much deeper than that. She wanted us to feel that we didn't do anything to cause her death.

It read:

To everyone I love:

Well, I wasn't going to write a note, but I figured that was rude. I want you all to know I appreciate the help you gave, but I just couldn't accept it. It's something that is wrong with me, no one else. No one could have done anything. Mom, Dad, thank you for 17 years of living. Thank you for all you gave me. Brian, Karen, Michelle — thank you for caring for me and watching out for me. And to all my friends who I turned to (you know who you are), thank you, thank you, thank you. I love you all. Pray for me so hopefully I will go to heaven. And as the song goes, "Just think of me and I'll be there."

Love, Denise

P.S. Please don't think you should have said, "I love you" one more time. I know you all love me, but I don't love myself. Remember the good times. Think of how happy I will be. I love you all. I'll miss you.

Someone heard Denise tell one of her friends, only weeks before her death, that she threw away her journals. Looking back, we know she didn't want people to blame themselves. That's why she remained in an upbeat mood during the month leading up to her death. She knew she was going to die and the pain was going to end, but she also didn't want to die on bad terms with anyone.

"At least I don't have to worry about her anymore," Mom would say at one point. Because Denise had tried to end her life five months before, Mom had been very concerned about whether my sister would attempt suicide again. Now the worrying was over.

On Saturday morning, my parents and Karen set off for the funeral home to pick out a casket. The wake would be Monday and the funeral Tuesday. I stayed behind and went for a run. As I ran down Oswego Road, part of one of my favorite routes, I felt like someone had turned the world on its side and didn't bother to tell me so I could adjust. I was definitely off balance. And it was another rainy day, typical for March in the Midwest.

When I returned to the house, I took a shower. As I turned the water off and combed my wet hair, I heard the doorbell. I pulled a T-shirt over my head and wrapped a towel around my waist. At the door stood one of my parents' neighbors with a very sad look on his face. He came to talk to my parents who still weren't home. Neither of us knew what to say.

When my family returned from the funeral home, Mom and Karen jokingly told me about the casket "showroom" with the caskets on wheels. Denise's would be a simple gray one. We dropped clothes off for her body at the funeral home: a favorite sweater, running shoes, and jeans. Mom toyed with adding Denise's favorite hat, one made in Guatemala that Denise loved, but decided she wanted to keep it. We added a shoebox of items including photos and some dog hair from Chaos, Karen's German Shepherd.

What we didn't realize was that Denise's body was very badly damaged. Her clothes and box of mementos were placed inside the casket with the body bag containing her remains.

We drove to Assumption Cemetery in Winfield, the first of two cemeteries we planned to visit. Mom wanted Denise buried in a Catholic cemetery. Assumption Cemetery is a twenty-minute drive from my parents' house. It rained the whole time we were there. A man showed us the open plots on the map, and we selected one under a tree.

The phone rang the rest of the day. I began calling Denise's friends so they knew when the funeral would be.

"Why didn't she call me if she needed to talk? She knew she could have called me," one boy wondered. I had no answers for him although I could feel his sadness. Denise had liked him a lot and I'd heard her mention his name often.

The October before, Mom had told us we couldn't tell anyone about Denise's first attempt because Denise didn't want anyone to know about it. In fact, my journal entry for the day she swallowed the aspirin, October 28, 1992, reads:

I'm supposed to say she has a bleeding ulcer, but Kim (one of my roommates) was there when I was on the phone and heard some of it so I told her. I feel bad, but I did need to tell someone.

When Denise died, Mom said, "Tell everyone. Maybe we can help someone else." We told her story again and again, looking for clues in talking and asking questions as we went along. Some families choose to protect the deceased, but Denise had chosen a very public way to die. We had no choice but to be open about her death.

There were so many people to tell. Most of my friends were away at college, but I found Laura, my high school locker partner, at home for the weekend, and she came over that night. The NCAA basketball tournament was on the little television sitting on the kitchen counter near the table where we sat. California was beating Duke as the Bears went on to become the Cinderella team of the "Big Dance" that year. Life didn't stop because Denise died.

The Naperville Sun, which at that time published three times a week, had run a story about Jane Doe walking in front of a train. Laura told me how she and her mom were reading the article and talking about the girl who died. Little did they know it was my sister.

Mom and I had stayed up all night talking and going through Denise's stuff. We didn't sort through it to get rid of it; we were only looking for answers. There had to be something to give us a clue.

My Sunday, March 21, 1993, journal reads:

I just want all of this over...There is this huge gaping hole in Denise's life that we don't understand... I miss Denise...I totally took her for granted. I called The Daily News and Brian (one of the editors) didn't say much. I wanted him to. I wanted to talk. He should know by now, but maybe he doesn't know. I wish they (my co-workers) would call me.

The principal opened Denise's high school that Sunday so students who needed help had somewhere to turn. He had called the day before while I was home alone and told me about this. He remembered me for my running. Did he even know my sister? I wondered. I was angry that people were going in on the weekend on account of her. The high school counselor called the house and asked me to stop by the school to talk because she also had been my counselor.

The group of us standing in the office was somewhat uncomfortable. I remarked how Denise used to cut my hair, and one of the counselors made a comment about how when someone dies, we don't think about those little things we have lost. Instead, we focus on the person as a whole and her personality traits such as humor or happiness. Those little things, like Denise cutting my hair, are just as important, she pointed out.

That Sunday night, Aunt Jeannette (Dad's sister) and Uncle Wally came to the house and brought dinner. We laughed and talked about my sports reporting. I had brought copies of *The Daily News* and showed them off. Denise should have been there.

The wake finally came Monday. When we drove to the funeral home, I thought about Wil-O-Way Park as we went by it. Sometimes Denise and I had gone there to play. It was also the same park she and her friends went to "throw the pigskin around." Not anymore.

Another friend of mine, J.J., was the first person to show up. She was early, but I was glad to see her. As we stood and talked, we heard Mom cry out from the viewing room where she was seeing the casket for the first time. We stayed in the back and watched. The silence was almost unbearable.

The list of people who showed up was endless. Cousins, teachers, friends' parents, and many I didn't know. The line to talk to Mom, who stood in front of the casket, wound around the chairs and out of the room. She stood up there in her blue jumpsuit and told Denise's story over and over. A boy I didn't know cried openly at the kneeler in front of her casket. Dad said the boy had worked with Denise at the retirement home where she was a food server. I had never seen so many men cry in my life. Pictures blanketed the casket, and we played some of Denise's favorite music tapes. The funeral home set up a bulletin board where we placed a few mementos representing Denise and cards everyone could fill out with their memories of her. Following the funeral, they were placed in the casket (Dad made copies for us to keep).

My card demonstrated my anger during the days following her death. I didn't realize until later that this outburst was typical of the suicide bereaved. Immediately, we look for a scapegoat, something or someone to blame for the death.

It read:

My sister dreaded going to school because so many people hurt her emotionally, and she didn't have the strength to rise above it. That insensitivity of others hurt Denise so much that she turned inward. There was so much to Denise that many didn't know about such as her love for older people, compassion for military veterans, interest in old movies, and willingness to be there for others, although they didn't seem to be there for her. And now she can't come back.

It rained as we drove home that night.

My Monday, March 22, 1993, journal entry reads:

Denise's wake is over. I told the school counselor how I am mad at some of the students for the way they treated her, and she seemed upset by that. It was weird. I know how those words from long ago hurt Denise. And tonight I read a note to Denise from her friend when I was opening cards. I didn't realize I shouldn't have read it and now I feel bad. Could Denise see me do that? Breakfast in the morning with Virginia at Grandma Sally's Pancake Restaurant, but I was so out of it because Denise's wake was 2:00 p.m. to 9:00 p.m. I cried when I saw people. And there were so many people! ...And teachers and old neighbors. It was neat to see them, but why under those circumstances? ...But she's gone, and I never realized how pretty she was until she was gone.

March 23, 1993, after the funeral:

I cried during parts of the funeral and screamed at Denise. Seeing so many people and Dad crying so hard really hurt me. There's got to be some good out of all this.

I had never seen Dad cry. He wasn't one to cry, and it amazed me that he wept openly and grabbed Denise's casket.

Mom brought their priest to the funeral home instead of going to church for the service. When he referred to Denise as "Linn," Mom told me she only corrected him because she was afraid I was going to fall off the couch laughing. It wasn't a good laugh, but I couldn't control it.

The music started as everyone walked by the casket one last time. The choir teacher at the high school had offered the services of some of his students to sing "Amazing Grace," "Be Not Afraid," and "On Eagle's Wings." I didn't know most of the people who filed by the casket. We were afraid to look at each other.

After all the people in the overflowing room had paid their last respects to Denise, we were given a few minutes alone with her. I cried and my brother wrapped his arm around me. We walked outside where we saw everyone lined up on the street by their cars or standing on the sidewalk, waiting for Denise to come out. The funeral director later told my parents he had never seen that happen before and that it was a wonderful tribute to Denise.

In the first car behind the hearse, we looked back and saw the line of cars as we drove up the hill on Mill Street.

"Well, Denise got to stop traffic one last time," Mom said as the cars drove through the red light by the high school.

It was cold and wet at the cemetery as we formed circles around the casket. Denise's friend Kristy stood next to me.

My parents asked everyone back to the house to eat after the funeral, although a few of her friends chose to stay by the casket after we drove away. The workers, ready to lower her body into the ground, waited in the background.

Many people had dropped food off that morning, and one woman had brought a bag of plates and napkins. She rang the doorbell and walked away, leaving a card and a paper bag behind. She didn't know Denise, but her son was the same age.

Mom invited all of Denise's friends (I thought she didn't like these people? Why were there so many of them? I had no idea who they were) upstairs to Denise's room. It remained relatively unchanged. She had never been really neat, and piles of laundry sat in one area. The students stood and stared. I knew most of them had probably not experienced any death, much less that of someone their own age. I made a joke about an Elvis Presley tape, but people only laughed nervously. Mom pointed out a few things as well. Denise was not coming back, and we knew they could feel that by the somber looks on their faces.

I didn't stay at the house long, however. The journalism teacher at the high school had asked me to come by during the newspaper class because I was a journalism major and the students weren't sure how to handle Denise's death in the school paper. Some of the students didn't want to mention Denise's death because they knew she hadn't been really happy at the school. I realized that by not acknowledging her death in the newspaper would be denial that she died. I never saw what they printed though.

I returned home to find my family sitting around a kitchen table filled with half-empty dishes of food. What was I going to do at home? I wondered. I had to get out of there. Bob, a friend of mine from Ball State, drove up to get me. His dad had died of cancer only months before so he was there when I needed a friend most. He understood.

Bob arrived and I went to find Dad to say goodbye. "I love you," he said as we stood by the stairs to the basement. I couldn't recall ever hearing those words from him before. Death changes us all.

The rest of my entry for March 23, 1993, reads:

I'm back in Muncie and I'm so glad it's over, but it feels weird. I have so much to do, and I'm tired. I got some cards here, including one from The Daily News. I don't know how it'll be when I go over there. They really don't know anything.

Then I returned to my life on March 24, 1993:

Felt out of sync and out of place all day. It's hard getting anything done!...I don't think the people at The Daily News know how to treat my situation...

I attended all my classes that day. Classmates asked where I'd been. My professors had been notified about my sister's death. I sat in the back corner of one class, and the professor offered to let me sit by the door so I could leave if I needed to.

But I wanted everything to be normal again. My life had changed while all their lives remained the same. I had a midterm exam in almost every class to make up. They told me I could take them when I wanted, but I finished them the next week. What was the sense in waiting? I wasn't going to study.

At *The Daily News*, Mike, the editor, told me I didn't have to be there. I could take a few days off. What would I do with my time? I craved normalcy. And I had returned to school a very different person.

This is really where my story begins. The thought of being a sibling survivor of suicide made me shudder. I had no idea that in the weeks after Denise's death the shock would wear off, setting me into a deep sadness that she wasn't going to return. I also didn't know anything about grief (especially after suicide) because I'd only lost my grandfathers whom I didn't know very well.

That's why I wrote this book. If I can comfort a survivor who lost a sibling to suicide or help someone learn how to console a sibling survivor, I have done my job. And in the process, I have also honored my sister Denise.

Chapter Two
This is Grief?

The sun shone brightly the day after Denise's funeral. It was the first I'd seen of it since the day before her suicide. I walked over to the church to pick up my bicycle where I had left it after finding out she had died. I had to slowly pick up the pieces of my life. I didn't know what to expect or even what grief was, but I realized I had to somehow go on. Classes and *The Daily News* weren't going to stop for my loss.

Everything changed in my life, not just when I found out Denise had died, or in the next year, but every day of my life since her death in 1993. In the days, weeks, and months after her suicide, I didn't understand why I had to stop running one day and kneel down and cry, barely aware of a man running by me. Why was I so tired all the time? And why did I talk to Denise out loud and feel such a need to keep a connection to her? I thought people stared, that they knew something was wrong with me because my sister took her life.

Those who I thought were my good friends at *The Daily News* didn't want to talk about what I'd been through. They wanted the old Michelle to return, but I was slowly realizing she was gone.

I had planned to study at the University of Calgary the following fall on an exchange program and, suddenly, that wasn't possible. I knew I couldn't go that far away from my parents so soon. They had lost one child and they couldn't bear to have another across the border in Canada.

Why couldn't my parents grieve together? They each talked about Denise to me, but not to each other. I thought I was alone in experiencing this. How could I know this was typical and happened to other sibling survivors?

The house was too quiet. I had to leave and go to a track meet because I couldn't stand the silence. I wanted to hear Denise running up the stairs and shutting her bedroom door.

Our world became smaller because Denise's friends drifted away. Some of their parents didn't want them to have anything to do with us after Denise died. Could their children choose Denise's path as well? Or were the parents of Denise's friends afraid of hurting their children if they told them I had called?

Not only do we lose our loved one; we see parts of the deceased person lost or destroyed beyond our control. One of Karen's dogs chewed up Denise's Raggedy

Ann before Karen could save her. Another piece of Denise was gone since she and I had played Raggedy Anns much of our childhood together.

I also found it important to throw out my Western Civilization book (the class I'd been pulled out of to be told of her death) as soon as I took the final exam. I didn't want to be reminded of that day any more than my memory served me. When I had found the aspirin container in Denise's bedroom from her first suicide attempt, I threw it away as quickly as I could.

What did I do then? I started coping in the only way I'd ever known. After the spring semester at Ball State ended, I kept a journal of letters I wrote to Denise. I had so much to share with her about what she was missing.

Below are some excerpts from that letter:

May 12, 1993

Dear Denise,

I can't believe it's taken me this long to write to you. I've been that way with everyone though.

Today was Mom's birthday and, because you weren't here, I made the angel food cake. What a disaster! I thought the batter tasted gross but it could've had something to do with the stuffing I sampled beforehand. Then I put it in the wrong pan. Like I know anything about angel food cake! This was your job, not mine. Dad asked if I was the official baker now. It'll always be you, Denise Susanna, even if you're not here. The cake got really big, too. Bigger than yours, maybe?

The trains are driving me crazy. I hear them all the time. In Muncie, they don't bother me. Biking the other day, I got stuck in front of a freighter on River Road. And when I went biking this morning, each time I was on River Road, the gates were down and the lights were flashing. I hear planes a lot, too, but my plane memories are happy.

I'm watching the final episode of "Knot's Landing." "Quantum Leap" ended last week and "Wonder Years" last night. A few of your favorite shows.

Dad said this morning someone has been to the cemetery to see you, there are flowers there. It's weird. I wonder who it is who thinks of you besides us. And how do your friends go on? I saw Stephanie at a track meet at

North Central College last week and she said it's strange without you. At the same time, I feel like people have forgotten you. My temper is still short and I have the worst attitude at work. I got invited to a barbecue at J.J.'s yesterday but I couldn't go. I couldn't be social.

I don't know how to deal with talking about you when I meet new people, like at work. I feel strange saying you committed suicide, but what else do I say? It's just that people are uncomfortable with the topic. They're afraid to ask but I want to talk about you but then I make them uneasy.

By the way, your driver's license is suspended because Dad stopped payment on that speeding ticket of yours. I told that story and the hubcap story at work yesterday. Remember losing the hubcap on the way to the dentist and how I picked it up on the tollway on the way back? That was funny!

Dad bought some vanilla Kemp's frozen yogurt. You should be here eating it with me.

June 11, 1993

I'm in Colorado Springs at the Olympic Training Center for my internship. There's so much I want to tell you but it's hard to write. I don't know why. But then, maybe you are experiencing it all with me.

I'm meeting all these athletes, including two wrestlers. I want to tell you about them. They are from near us. I know you would be excited if you were here.

I went walking tonight. The peacefulness of a Friday night was wonderful. How could you give that up? I called Kristy because I needed someone to talk to. She understands. I dreamt you came back the other night. I was in a horrible mood the next morning, but I can't explain to people why. I just can't.

Sometimes when I'm sitting at my computer, I think about you in front of the train or the funeral. It's all so far away yet it will never go away.

June 14, 1993

I can't sleep and staring up at the sky and knowing you are up there is too eerie. I keep thinking of the funeral and the chain of events. How did we get through it?

I called home yesterday for a phone number and practically started crying on Dad. So many things seem so senseless. He told me I needed to go on. Running taught me how to get back up when I fall down, but I hurt so much that in some ways, I want to sit on the ground. Then, on the phone with Tris, I did cry. Did you see it? Are you here now? Do you know how much we are hurting? Do you regret what you did?

I thought about the Kane County Cougars games tonight and cheering for our favorite players. How could you just throw that memory away?

At the chili cook-off here Saturday, the gift shop had all these $4.00 T-shirts. I couldn't calculate how many to buy for Christmas gifts because you are gone. Then I saw the pins you collect. I wanted to buy you some so badly. But I can't. You aren't coming back. That hurts. Really hurts. Karen bought some baseball cards while I was at school and sent me some. She said she had to stop herself from buying you some. She said you have taken some of the little things of joy out of her life by killing yourself.

Although this letter to Denise helped me manage my loss, I had no control over what others said to me. The comments started from the moment I told people Denise died. I heard everything from Denise's life being a waste because she only lived seventeen years, to those who insisted I be strong for my parents. And then, after a few months, people started to tell me to get over it. A few people said nothing, which hurt just as much.

How were those comments supposed to make me feel? That it was a waste to have my sister around for seventeen years? Mom said that if she had known she would lose Denise at seventeen, she still would have had her again. Each life is worth so much, even when we don't have it as long as we expect to. This person, however, saw it sad that Denise didn't experience much life and had ended it prematurely.

One classic line many siblings hear is, "Be strong for your parents." What people forget is that the surviving sibling needs to take care of himself or herself first. If we are strong for our parents, what's left for ourselves? No one is going to take care of us.

At the funeral, I was told that the experience of losing my sister would make me a better writer. So, as writers, we should all experience death? I know she meant Denise's death would make me stronger and more compassionate, but that comment definitely didn't ease my pain. There is also, "Look for the silver lining in this death." Where is the silver lining when your sister has taken her life?

And the rumors. There are more rumors with suicides than other deaths. I was asked if she had been caught in a bad drug deal. I felt so insulted that this person, who had met Denise previously, would think that. A friend heard a parent at a high school athletic event say that Denise had been drunk at the spring dance. This was very difficult to believe, even if she knew she was going to die days later. After all, this was the same Denise who had experimented with alcohol at one point, but then shunned it in the last few years of her life. I felt tortured after this comment. I began to wonder how well I knew Denise because I hadn't seen her death coming. Again, rumors are bound to happen, especially with a public death. It's like playing Telephone where you start with a comment at one side of the room and by the time it's whispered to the other side, it has nothing to do with the original remark. People need something to talk about in our society. The juicier the story, the better.

Many people told me they knew Denise although I was sure they didn't. I had to understand they were affected by her death because she had opted to take her life. I wondered if they were really upset because she had died or because it made them feel guilty for their own failings.

Besides, I thought, if they were really her friends, where were they when she needed them? Or didn't she want them there? Some people just like to be part of the drama. It's important to know where one belongs in the scheme of events.

After Denise had been dead three months, someone told me to "get over it" because "so much time" had passed. People aren't educated on the grief experience so they think grief is done following a three-day bereavement leave from work. That person just wanted the old Michelle to come back and be the happy person who laughed so often. What he didn't realize, however, was that the old Michelle was gone. I could never return to who I was, even when I wanted to, just as I couldn't bring Denise back. I'm sure some of it had to do with ghosts in this person's own closet he chose not to cope with.

Someone also said, "You'll always be the same Michelle you were before your sister died. You'll like the same things and do the same things." I don't believe I had much of a reaction to that, but some time after hearing it, I realized I would never be the same Michelle again. Certain parts of my life lost their meaning. For instance, Denise and I loved baseball. We were big Chicago Cubs fans and one year subscribed to *Baseball Weekly* under the name "Michenise." When she died, I stopped following the sport.

The few games I went to brought strong waves of emotion, making them difficult to enjoy. I had to put together baseball standings almost every night at *The Daily News,* a constant reminder that my sister was no longer living. Even viewing highlights of games on television was hard. We used to buy baseball cards every year and, suddenly, it wasn't the same. Finally, three years after Denise died, I could watch and enjoy it again, but it won't ever be as it was. I don't watch it like I used to because there's no Denise with whom to share it.

Some summer nights we used to run out to the nearby grocery store to pick up frozen yogurt. I can still feel the warm night air as we drove home, listening to country music on the car radio. I see us sitting in the kitchen watching the Cubs play a late game in Los Angeles on the little black and white television as we ate our dessert. Yes, I have the memories, but I can't relive them with anyone else. Not having Denise to do those things with has changed me. It makes me sad, but death can alter the bereaved in many ways we don't control. Instead, the bereaved have to learn to rebuild and in that process they become someone new. Grief forces growth, even in ways not chosen.

As the days took us further from Denise's death, the comments continued. One friend couldn't believe I wanted to go to the train tracks to see where Denise died. Those tracks were part of my reality now. I also wanted to see where Denise was last alive. Then a man asked me if I knew how badly bodies are torn apart after pedestrian vs. train accidents.

Seven months after we lost Denise to suicide, Grandma Zurawski died. Someone told me, "Death comes in threes. Better watch out for your dog." As if losing two loved ones wasn't hard enough, this person had to suggest I might experience another death in the near future.

The most hurtful comment came over a year after my sister died when I dated a man who told me, "I can't empathize with you because I think you've let this go on too long." He added, "I think you like feeling guilty in a perverse way." Again, this is a classic example of how people who haven't been through grief perceive it. They think you only need a short time to grieve and you should never talk about the loved one or their death. All I ever wanted was someone to listen to me and be there when I needed to talk. I found it difficult with many people who hadn't been through any sort of loss in their lives though.

And there are others who choose to say nothing at all. This was the case with one teacher both Denise and I had in high school. After Denise's death, I heard he was having a hard time and took the day of her funeral off. I believed he would come to the wake or the funeral. I wanted to see him and talk to him myself, but he never showed. This left me perplexed so I wrote him a letter. I didn't get an answer. I really wanted to know what Denise was like in the classroom because my parents had been told she was very up and down. Her teachers hadn't been so worried about her schoolwork as much as they were worried about her. They knew she could do the work. Denise would get a 100 percent on one speech, beating out the boy from the speech team, but she wouldn't even hand in the next assignment.

I can't describe the hurt I felt when he didn't respond. I wondered if something was wrong with me. A year later, after talking to someone else about not hearing from the teacher, I wrote him another letter. That one also went unanswered. Then, having forgotten about it, my parents received a letter in the mail addressed to me. He had finally written, over two years later. In the letter, he apologized and told me he didn't want to deal with the sadness of Denise's suicide, as he had never been faced with such a loss before. He really liked having her in class and her death took him by surprise. We talked on the phone sometime after that and I finally could let go of the situation.

There was one other person I didn't hear from after Denise's death, a man who was a large source of support to me as a high school runner. I also expected him to attend the funeral. Other people even asked me if he had. People were as surprised as I was when I told them he failed to attend.

While in Colorado, someone suggested I write him a letter, and so I did. He wrote back and told me he had been dealing with some other issues in his life and had been confident that I had the support I needed. Hearing from him gave closure to the issue, but it still bothered me that he didn't acknowledge her death when it happened. It doesn't take much to send off a quick note or leave a phone message. I didn't expect him to sit down and spend time with me. I just wanted him to say he was aware of what happened, especially because he had influenced me so positively in high school. Instead, I quickly learned how difficult grief was for many people.

Why did I feel so alone on holidays? Why couldn't I have what everyone else had—a complete family? Easter, only weeks after Denise's death and days from her birthday, was very difficult. I was at Ball State, and Pat, from my church, invited me (as she did each year) to attend Mass and eat out with her family. It was sad for me as my family wasn't together, nor would we ever be in the same form again. I felt grouchy that afternoon, just wanting to return to my apartment. At the time, however, I had no idea why I felt so annoyed.

That first Christmas, as I put the tree up, it was hard deciding what to do with Denise's stocking. She had the best one. Mom made all of ours with lots of sequins. Each one is unique. While Brian, Karen, and I had felt stockings with a red and green motif, Denise's is blue and white with a gingerbread house and numerous colored sequins on it.

On that day, I sat down on the stairs in the basement and all I could do was look at her stocking. We couldn't put it up; that would be like we thought she was coming home, but it seemed ridiculous to let it sit in the box. The box won out.

The initial Christmas after Denise's death was the most difficult, especially because we had suffered twice in our family that year with the loss of my maternal grandmother. Suddenly, we had no Christmas plans. Karen and I helped her boss deliver gifts to needy families that year. We were looking for new meaning ourselves on a day we had always enjoyed so much. It took several years before we finally settled into a new routine.

Even the places important to me were altered. Assumption Cemetery became a part of my life. I know my sister is always near me but sometimes I find it essential to drive to the cemetery.

Denise's friend Kristy and I went there one early summer night in the months after Denise died. She hadn't been there since the funeral. The sun was setting and we stood by the grave, just talking about Denise's life. Later, we spotted a couple, just about 200 yards away. As we approached them, we saw they were drinking glasses of wine.

"We weren't sure if we should come over or not," we told them, but they welcomed us and said they felt the same way. The man's brother had died in a car accident and he had given them a bottle of wine before he died. They were there on the deceased brother's birthday, drinking the wine.

We wandered back to Denise's grave and talked more as the sun continued to set, only scrambling to leave when we saw the gates were about to be shut for the night. Somehow, we didn't really think about the fact that we were sitting in the cemetery. It was just another place. Perhaps it was comforting because Denise was there.

I also found it necessary to visit the spot at the train tracks where she had died, despite opposition from people who didn't understand my need to see it. I felt an urge to go to the train tracks twice: once with Kristy to see the power of a train go by and the second time on December 23, 1993, the first Christmas without Denise. I had to be at the place she last was before she died, knowing she wouldn't be with us for the holidays.

And what about her belongings? What did we do with a room filled with Denise's life? We had a difficult time figuring out what to do with her stuffed animals and school papers. What about the clothes? Why did we save them? She wasn't coming back. Why did we get rid of them? We kept what we wanted and felt would help us remember her. We have her writings, drawings, and some of her favorite clothes. It's hard to throw away each item, however, as I felt I was throwing away a part of her. I would stare at her writing one last time. She'll always remain in my memories, but there are times that we want a little more to keep.

Sadly, some items that meant so much to her didn't invoke any feelings for us. I threw all her dental appointment cards away. In my eyes, I didn't understand why she kept them anyway. Mom, Karen, and I kept the clothes we wanted to wear. We gave her stuffed animals to Kristy who was then pregnant with her daughter. All that remains of Denise's life is a trunk filled with the personal possessions that might not have meant the most to her, but do to us.

Grief isn't going to be over in one day. Understanding suicide doesn't happen in a period of hours. It was my experiences, both of coping within myself and with others, that showed me I would be stronger when I came out on the other side.

Do They Have Bad Days in Heaven?

Chapter Three
One of 48,000

*(Author's note: When this book was original written and published in
2001, there were approximately 31,000 known suicides per year in the
United States. Up until 1999, there had been long-term trends of decline in
suicide and about a 2% yearly uptick since then. The new edition reflects
the current numbers as published for 2018, the latest year that data was
available for at the time of publication.)*

We've all heard the jokes. Sometimes we even laugh about it ourselves. Once someone told me that he would rather slit his wrists than deal with his parents at home. Or we know someone who makes a drastic change in his life and people wonder, "Does he want to commit suicide?" But what exactly is suicide? Usually, until we lose a loved one to it, we aren't interested in what the word actually means. I know I wasn't.

Many dictionaries define suicide as "the act of killing oneself purposely." It comes from the Latin words *sui*, which means "self," and *caedere*, which means "to kill."

I don't remember learning what suicide was, as I'm sure most of us don't. I do, however, recall a boy in eighth grade telling me to "commit suicide with a Swatch guard" (the plastic covering for the famous watch that kept it from getting scratched) and two classmates attempting suicide. Those who tried to end their lives always returned to school from the psychiatric unit of the hospital when the insurance money ran out. It didn't matter whether or not they were healed, they were sent back to reality.

In high school, a boy I knew died, severely injuring his body in the process. I had met him in junior high when I was a student council member who showed new students around. For reasons I never understood, other kids made fun of the shape of his head, calling him "pear," and he transferred to a different high school. In health class my sophomore year, our teacher asked us to write on a piece of paper whether we had ever thought about ending our lives. I know I wrote yes. Although I could never go through with it, many times I was angry with others and thought it might be a way to hurt them. He recorded our answers and, not surprisingly, most people said yes.

It is estimated that 1.4 million American adults (over the age of eighteen) attempted to die by suicide in 2018. When faced with difficult situations, we believe it would be easier to die by suicide than cope with our fears, perceived failures, or loneliness. Most people, however, do face their problems and the suicide attempt becomes a part of their past.

Suicide isn't a recent phenomenon. It has been with us as long as there has been life. In the First Egyptian Period, suicide was considered to be an option if one was not happy with his or her life. Later, the ancient Greeks were the first to view suicide as a negative force. They believed that people who died by suicide weren't of right mind, and that the ghosts of suicide victims were vengeful. The Greeks also considered suicide to be a sin against the gods.

In the eighteenth century, laws were enacted in Europe (and eventually in the United States) to make suicide a crime. Those who died by suicide were dragged through the streets and stoned, or they were buried at a crossroads as a sign of disgrace. Families were stripped of their belongings and ostracized because they were considered accessories to the crime.

By the nineteenth century, suicide became associated with insanity rather than crime. However, laws against suicide remained on the books, as did the stigma associated with it. That taboo revolved around the concept that the deceased were mentally ill. This stigma came from society's fear of mental illness and that the "disease" was contagious. Often, families didn't report suicide deaths to save themselves from judgment and ostracism.

That was the case in my own family. In the 1960s, my mother's uncle died by suicide. She wasn't allowed to talk about the experience because he would be denied a Catholic burial. I found this out the day of Denise's wake.

Today, the Catholic Church still calls suicide a sin, but the newest edition of the *Catechism of the Catholic Church*, published in 1994, still skirts around the issue, according to Fr. Charles, Rubey who has worked extensively with the suicide bereaved, saying that, "God judges us negatively when we act out of malice. People who die by suicide act out of pain, not malice."

The bereaved can't be denied a Christian burial now, no matter how their loved one died. In the often-quoted words of Pope Francis, "Who am I to judge?"

There are many books available now that describe the different views of suicide in respect to different religious traditions.

Beyond the stigma, many suicide bereaved wrestle with the question of why their loved ones chose to die this way. What drove them to do it? Were they mentally ill? Were drugs and alcohol involved?

There is no easy answer. As each person is unique, so is each suicide. According to Dr. McIntosh and the National Center for Health Statistics, approximately 48,000 people end their lives by suicide each year in the United States. However, those are only the reported cases. Others may be listed as accidents or natural causes to protect the deceased and the family. The World Health Organization estimates that 800,000 people die by suicide each year in the world or one person every forty seconds.

We also know more women attempt suicide than men, but men are more likely to die in their attempts, a 3:1 ratio. Men accounted for 78.1% of all suicides in 2018. Men are still more likely to choose firearms to end their lives.

We lose more middle-aged men to suicide than any other age group at a rate of 20.1 per 100,000 rate. In contrast, suicide is the second leading cause of death for people ages fifteen to twenty-four and their rate is 14.5 per 100,000.

As my sister was one of those young people, in my early years as a bereaved person, I thought teen suicide was the most important issue. However, now that I'm older and see how many middle-aged men we lose, I also see that many of these teens are losing not just their fathers, but role models like uncles and other important people in their lives. Often, teen suicide is the issue people put out in front because of the loss of life in many ways before has really begun. Yet we forget that when people are exposed to suicide, it increases their own risk. How much it increases their risk, we still don't know, but as I have said before, suicide becomes part of your life in a close and personal way. It's not something that happened to the family down the street. It happened in your family and can happen again.

Many suicides occur in the spring when it is difficult to witness the "rebirth" of life on trees and flowers beginning to bloom. Western states have more suicides, perhaps because of geographic isolation and lack of close proximity to mental health care.

Some factors leading to suicide might include isolation, hopelessness, helplessness, any sort of loss (job, relationship, financial), illness (physical or mental), peer pressure, abuse (alcohol, sexual), major life change (could be related to a loss as well), violence, LGBTQ issues as someone struggles to feel accepted in society, and family history of suicide. Other contributors include culture, personality, and physiological factors (e.g., low levels of serotonin). Oftentimes, suicide involves a combination of factors.

According to most suicidologists, mental illness usually plays a role in suicide. People suffering from mental illnesses (including schizophrenia and bipolar disorder, also known as manic depressive illness) are more likely to die by suicide. Depression is often a factor, especially among those people who think their lives are worthless. Oddly enough, depressed people are more likely to take their lives when they begin to come out of the depression as they have the energy to follow through with the act. Denise fit this description as she was in relatively good spirits in the months leading up to her death because she had everything planned and she knew her pain would end.

Many times, suicide involves drug and/or alcohol problems. Approximately two out of three suicides involve substance abuse. Professionals point to a correlation between alcoholics and those who die by suicide because both groups have difficulty maintaining rewarding relationships. Drinking allows alcoholics to withdraw from pain or rejection, just as those who die by suicide choose death over life for the same reason. The deceased might abuse drugs and alcohol as a direct or indirect way of choosing suicide. They also could abuse alcohol, which works as a disinhibitor (thus the reason people think they are immortal when they are drinking), helping them to decide to die and follow through with it.

Others choose suicide because they think they have failed their culture and society. In this scenario, people with self-critical personalities are most at risk. It is not uncommon for an adolescent who's been a straight-A student to decide to end his or her life after getting his or her first B in a class. Or the adolescent could be upset that his or her parents are going to divorce. Similarly, the self-critical adult who's lost a job might choose suicide as well. That same personality might end his or her life after a failed marriage.

Suicide, however, is a combination of factors, not just one life event. Some people might not be equipped to manage the stress they feel from their family, job, school, or community. These stressors also might drop down on the person at one time and he or she might not know how to cope with them all. I've heard many people say the one who died by suicide was "overly responsible" or "the caregiver" for all of his or her friends. It was easier to solve everyone else's problems and put one's own difficulties on the back burner.

While being LGBTQ is much more accepted than when this book was first published in 2001, it's still a societal factor as people feel the stigma and challenge of being accepted in society. LGBTQ people sometimes choose suicide because they're unable to work through their feelings and/or they're fearful of confronting family members about their sexual orientation. They also might have been ostracized by people in their lives.

Illnesses that cause a loss of control lead others to suicide. Examples include eating disorders (anorexia and bulimia), chronic illness, and terminal cancer. These people prefer to end life on their own terms. People with eating disorders might fear having to fight food the rest of their lives.

Suicide is also considered a heroic effort by certain segments of society. Political extremists, so-called "suicide bombers," attach bombs to their bodies and then walk into crowded areas, dying by suicide and killing those around them for their cause.

In some cases, people who take their own life might not truly understand what death is either; they somehow think it's not final, but instead a beginning, and they won't die. The Heaven's Gate Cult best exemplifies this. The cult members died by suicide in 1997, thinking the Hale-Bopp Comet was really a spaceship coming to pick them up. By dying, they would lift out of their bodies or "shells" and be transported to the ship.

Finally, indirect suicide is defined as purposely putting oneself into a risky situation. Crossing busy streets during rush hour is one example. Or "suicide by cop," when people maneuver themselves into situations to die at the hands of the police.

The reasons people choose to die come from inside themselves, their outside environment, and their personal experience. Each death is as unique as the person, and it's much easier to record who dies by suicide than why.

Since Denise's death, I've searched for clues as to why my sister took her life. How did the rape affect her state of mind? We also contemplated the possibility that Denise might have been pregnant and was afraid to tell anyone. Or had she feared that she could never enjoy food like most people? What about her depression? Had she felt apprehension about it returning in the future?

I often wonder if Denise had a healthy attitude toward or a preoccupation with death. My parents both came from large families and, as we grew up, their aunts and uncles began to die. Denise always went with Mom and Dad to the funerals and enjoyed walking around the cemeteries and seeing the graves of relatives. Every gerbil that died in our house received a funeral in the backyard with crosses made of sticks. Was she more comfortable with death than any of us could imagine or understand? However, we also we were taught that death was part of the life cycle and it wasn't shielded from us.

Maybe it was something else. In the mid-1980s, Denise seemed to develop a sense of isolation as she watched the family drift apart. Karen went to college. Brian moved out. I spent most of my time at school or running, then I went to college. In addition, my family was jolted when Dad's job was eliminated, forcing him to retire. Suddenly, he was home every day, and Mom went back to work.

Did living in Naperville play a part in her unhappiness? Naperville is an upper-middle class town thirty miles west of Chicago. We moved there in 1974, a year before Denise was born. When my parents had our house built, only 20,000 people resided in the sleepy suburb.

It's a beautiful place that had a small-town atmosphere. Everyone knew each other in Naperville. In the neighborhoods around town, parents felt safe letting their children run around freely. We swam at Centennial Beach, an old quarry converted into a large swimming pool in the 1930s, which we biked to from our parents' house. Downtown is the Riverwalk with long, winding red brick paths that look endless.

As time wore on and the Illinois Research and Development Corridor grew, Naperville's face changed. When Denise died, the population hovered near 100,000. It had become too big. The pressure to succeed and "keep up with the Joneses" also escalated. The real Naperville became buried as it grew.

I still think about the outward perfection of Naperville and other suburban towns like it. As far as the facade goes, no one has problems. Once you reach in deeper, you get a sense of what isn't right. I wonder what Denise's perception was of Naperville. Here she lived in this place where you weren't supposed to have any problems, but hers were serious. Did she feel inadequate? Did she think she didn't belong? Did that contribute to her decision to end her life?

While Denise felt anger from the change in that atmosphere, she also dreaded my parents eventually moving from the only house she knew. The few writings we have from her reveal she wanted to cling to a past she couldn't regain. Outwardly, she wanted to move ahead to the distant future, but she couldn't cope with what came in between: today.

Shortly after Denise died, I received a letter from a childhood friend. Christine, Denise, and I had spent many hours playing with our Barbie dolls. We built houses out of boxes and wagon trains from picnic baskets. In the letter, Christine reminded me how easy it all had been when we were young:

You know, our Barbies were perfect. They always had friends, they were beautiful, successful, and happy. Always happy unless we made them sad. When they were sad though, we had the power to change the circumstances and make it all work out. How simple. Who knew it would get so complex...I wish things were as easy as the lives of our Barbies and when we got sick of the problems, just change the course of events.

I echo Christine's words, how simple it seemed. We had no idea how difficult life would become for Denise. Her suicide was a combination of all the above factors, yet we'll still never really know why she ended her life. Now she's a number, one of 48,000.

Do They Have Bad Days in Heaven?

Chapter Four
A Myriad of Emotions

Survivor. How I hated that word. Because my sister ended her life on her own terms, I was thrown into a category that I didn't understand, nor wanted any part of. I'd always thought survivor meant someone walked away from a plane crash or a car accident, not that they had "survived" the suicide of a loved one.

A suicide survivor is any person who loses someone he or she cares about to a suicide death. The language around this word has changed since I first published this book. Now we use the words "survivor of suicide loss" or "bereaved" and call someone who attempts suicide a "survivor" or "attempter." I will use "suicide bereaved" from this point on to describe someone who loses someone to suicide although sometimes people still say "suicide survivor" for the bereaved. It all changed for me when I began to speak overseas where they used different terms than us in the United States and it began to cause confusion.

We become suicide bereaved if a loved one dies by suicide (our sibling, parent, child, spouse) or if the suicide deeply affected someone close to us (our spouse's sibling, our child's best friend, other important people in our orbit of life). Dr. Edwin Shneidman, often called the founder suicidology, created the first estimate that for every suicide, at least six people become survivors of suicide loss. While we believe the number six to be too low, we also believe that Shneidman was referring to the immediate family as there are several stories he used, including one (that he shared with me not long before his death) about who was due financial reward in a case he consulted on regarding a cemetery double-burying bodies.

However, more recent research (done by Julie Cerel and her colleagues both at the University of Kentucky and around the world) suggests that for each suicide, 135 are exposed to suicide, however, this doesn't mean that all these people will have an emotional attachment to the person who died by suicide.

When I think of six people "closely affected" by my sister's suicide, I know six is far too low. There are five of us in the immediate family alone. Add her good friends, relatives, classmates, co-workers, and anyone else who knew Denise, including my friends who reacted strongly to her death. What about the neighbors? Her teachers? Where does the list end? How long is this list for others who have died by suicide? I sometimes wonder, of those people whose lives were touched by Denise, how many still think of her years later? One never stops being a survivor of suicide loss.

Many years ago, the bereaved who experienced a suicide were forced into silence. The stigma that suicide was embarrassing and could ruin a family's reputation ran high. This silence led to many mental and physical problems because survivors feared outwardly expressing their grief in a consistent manner of bereavement. Shame and guilt overwhelmed those left behind.

It wasn't until the late 1950s when the Los Angeles Suicide Prevention Center began what are called psychological autopsies — questioning the bereaved to get a feel for the deceased's thinking in his or her last days — that anyone began to understand survivors had a need to express their feelings about the death. In the 1970s, support groups (including HEARTBEAT and Survivors of Suicide) surfaced to provide survivors the opportunity to talk about their experiences and emotions with other survivors. Such support groups created a safe environment to talk and share. Today, we are offer people many coping mechanisms, not just support groups, to help people walk their journey of suicide grief. For some people, therapy works well and for others they are looking for ideas of how to travel the road, how to remember their loved one, how to cope. I explore that much more in my book, *Rocky Roads: The Journeys of Families through Suicide Grief.*

For instance, even though the stigma of suicide has lessened since the first version of this book was published, why do so many suicides still go unreported? Is it because the stigma is still evident in the actions of many people? Those on the outside of the situation back away from the bereaved to ward off their own fears of death and "self murder." The bereaved begin to blame themselves because they had a suicide in their family. Expressions such as "she committed suicide" or "he killed himself" are still used today. To avoid the stinging feeling that comes with those words especially "commit" because it connotates it was a crime, I now use "died by suicide." Some people prefer "suicided" or "completed suicide" although to use "complete" makes it sound like one "tried" before.

We have a long way to go in changing our perception, but we can begin with the way the media portray suicide. If the media glorify or romanticize suicide, suicidal people might believe their choice is one that will make them idols when they are gone. If the media stigmatize a suicide, the bereaved find themselves stuck in a closet, unable to come out and get the help and support they need. We couldn't cover up Denise's death when it was on the front page of the local newspaper. If we had the option to cover it up, I don't know what the choice would have been. My family holds a long record of secrecy, and I'm sure my parents would have toyed with the idea just to avoid the stigma. For our grief, it was better we had no choice and faced it head on, stigma and all.

Because suicide leaves a stigma to cope with, it also changes the lives of the bereaved. Five years after Denise's death, someone asked me how Denise's suicide had changed my life. My first thought was that I didn't have any choice but to go on because the world didn't stop on account of Denise's death, but all I could remember was lethargy because when my sister walked in front of a train, my life was already full with work and school.

When the Ball State basketball team lost in the first round of the NCAA Tournament, I thought I was going to have time for myself again. Instead, my plate overflowed with the start of my grief journey along with my daily responsibilities. I worked the three weeks after school ended that spring before driving to Colorado Springs, Colorado, for my journalism internship at the Olympic Training Center. I started the following fall semester as sports editor of *The Daily News* while taking a full load of classes. Life became a constant struggle to stay afloat. I wasn't aware of how this hectic lifestyle was affecting me until I left the newspaper in January 1994, and those close to me said how glad they were that I quit.

To help us understand the path we have embarked upon, we must know the difference between grief, bereavement, and mourning. Grief causes us to feel out of control in our lives, and the less we know about it, the more difficult it'll be. It's the emotional response to suffering a loss and has been compared to a physical injury or illness. Chronic grief is grief that continues to manifest itself because it's never truly worked through. Just as a chronically ill person can't get better, a person suffering from chronic grief won't improve. We must let grief happen. Bereavement is the reaction to the loss. Mourning is our outward expression of grief, the period in which we acknowledge the death of our loved one.

When analyzing the grieving process, there are three main factors that determine the intensity of grief.

They are:

1. What else was going on in our lives at the time of the death?

2. What was our relationship with the deceased?

3. What type of death was it?

Professionals might add the level of our social support, socio-economic factors, and how we've handled previous losses in our lives.

What else was going on when the person died? Was life simply humming along or were there stressors with work, school, or other relationships? All these will affect the grieving process, just as working for the newspaper affected mine. I often wonder, if I hadn't been so tired from the basketball season, would I have had more strength to better carry me through those difficult months? Instead, my exhaustion was obvious as I spent most days wanting to fall asleep at my office desk during my internship.

If we were attached to the person, it obviously will have a significant impact on our lives. I considered myself close to my sister and, because she was so near to me in age, we were like friends, which complicates the grief process further. I will address this in Chapter Six, which specifically discusses sibling suicide loss.

Suicide grief is easily distinguished from other types of death because of the fact that the person ended his or her life. He or she made a decision that he or she didn't want to live, setting up complicated grief work for those left behind. The suicide bereaved can't blame a drunk driver or the cancer. Many times, I wished there was something tangible I could hold responsible because it was so hard to accept that my sister couldn't cope anymore. Someone even suggested it was the anti-depressant, Prozac, she took that drove her to suicide. We liked that answer because it provided us with a convenient target for blame. Denise's Prozac bottle wasn't empty though, and toxicology reported that no Prozac was found in her blood. She had stopped taking it some time before her death. Still, we yearned for something to blame, for some assurance that we weren't responsible for her death.

Also, with a suicide, the grieving process is complicated because the yearning for answers is so great. As a result, the grief path becomes longer, more twisted, and less defined. I've heard that losing someone to suicide is like having a heated argument with someone who has the last word.

Some research, however, has classified many of the suicide grief reactions as the same of those of any sudden death. There is no opportunity for anticipatory grief in an accident or suicide death. Anticipatory grief is when one has a terminal illness and the family or friends watch the person's decline. Because they grieve prior to the loved one's death, they have the opportunity to say goodbye. In an accident or suicide, however, the death is almost always a shock. Often, it's only in hindsight that suicide bereaved see clues they missed or ignored.

The suicide bereaved, especially those who witnessed the suicide or found the body, might experience post traumatic stress disorder (PTSD). This is most frequently associated with veterans returning home from war and experiencing flashback-like aftereffects. In their mind, a backfiring bus becomes gunfire, and they drop to the ground when they hear loud noises. The suicide bereaved might replay images of the loved one shooting himself or herself, or his or her body hanging in the basement, like a horror movie. It's important to seek professional help if one is experiencing PTSD.

Suicide grief doesn't make the bereaved immune to suicide themselves. It's a myth that if someone dies by suicide, no more family members will follow a similar path. Taking one's life has become reality for the family; a feasible option. Survivors might think about suicide subconsciously by walking across the street without looking (this happened to me once at Ball State). Those feelings can also stem from trying to connect with the person who died.

What we believe about life after death will play a part in grieving. Many of us believe in a higher power and feel comfortable knowing our loved one is now with that higher power, or we might not fear death anymore because we know we'll see him or her again. My family talks about Denise going fishing with Grandpa Linn, who died in 1983, and greeting Grandma Zurawski and Karen's dog, Chaos, when they died.

This death could make us question our beliefs. How could our higher power allow such an awful event to happen? There many things we questions after a loss, especially a suicide loss, and there's nothing wrong with that. Walk the road, ask, and one day you'll be surprised when you find an answer or maybe you'll forget that it had been important to you to ask at one time.

I had stopped praying daily not long before Denise died. I don't know why, but when I found out she died, I immediately thought I caused her death because I'd quit praying and because I hadn't been attending church. It took some time for me to start praying again. I kept thinking, "Denise is gone so what does it matter now?" Those thoughts eventually subsided, and I found myself, much to my relief, talking to Denise and feeling like she was listening to me.

Those who don't believe in a higher power might have a more difficult time dealing with their grief. They have no thoughts of an afterlife to cling to. They believe life ends with the last breath, that there is nothing beyond. This is a very personal issue and one that we can share only with those whom we feel most comfortable.

Universally among grief, however, there exist feelings and emotions one might endure. Listed below are typical reactions that those grieving a suicide death might experience. There is no "accepted order" to go through these; some survivors might not experience them at all. It's not limited to those listed either. One could also feel anxiety, longing for the person who died, fear, rejection, forgetfulness, lack of concentration and control, emptiness, a lack of sense of belonging, sudden mood swings, less interest in activities enjoyed before the death, sadness, and countless other emotions. The list is endless. Please note that many of these are the same symptoms as depression. These can be felt at the same time or separately. We endure a myriad of emotions in grief and none of our paths will be alike. Fortunately, awareness will help us cope and remove some of the isolation we feel.

Shock

Immediately after the suicide, the bereaved will usually experience shock. This comes from the unexpectedness of the death. It's this shock, or numbness, that acts as a padded wall to soften the blow of the loss. That's what gets us through the burial plans and funeral. It's also the shock that keeps us from putting the deceased into past tense. Until we can recover from this numbness, we talk as if our loved one is still here. "We always go to the store together," we might say. As we integrate the death into our lives, we start to refer to the deceased in the past tense. Shock usually wears off within the first few weeks following the suicide.

Denial

Denial can be part of the shock when, initially, we can't accept that the person isn't coming back. Denial also can grow like a malignancy if we continually insist that the person will return, even weeks or months after the death. Comments from those in denial include, "We need to save some dinner for her because she'll be home later," or "We need to buy Christmas gifts for him." Denial is also waking up in the morning and forgetting what happened to the loved one or "seeing" him or her on the street. The survivor might admit the person has died but will instead deny the death was suicide. If denial continues for a long period of time, professional help must be sought to work through the avoided issues relating to the loved one and/or the death.

Guilt

Guilt plagues many survivors. They will contemplate what they could have said or done differently to have kept the person alive. They might wonder why they didn't pick up on clues forewarning them of the suicide or think they failed to make the person want to live. They might feel bad for enjoying life while their loved one is no longer with them.

While many let this guilt fester, they also often think they could have changed events, but would that guarantee the person staying alive? No one will ever know what could have happened "if only" things were different. Suicide is the ultimate could have, would have, and should have. We can't go back and do it over. People who have died by suicide were coping with much more than we could have ever changed with one statement. Happiness is an inside job. No matter what we say or how we try to help, that person needed something we couldn't provide. There comes a time when we have to accept that we have done all we can.

Guilt might overwhelm survivors because they feel relief that the loved one is free from his or her pain. In our society, we emphasize living a long life and fearing death. People feel badly expressing relief because they're afraid of what others will think. They could also worry because the deceased's problems were hidden; most people didn't know about them. How can you tell your friend that you feel relief that your loved one is out of pain when your friend didn't know about your loved one's difficulties?

Survivors suffer from guilt for feeling good and laughing after the death. They think they need to feel sad all the time because the loved one is gone. It seemed strange when I felt good for the first time in days, weeks, even months. I was invited to a barbecue with my Daily News co-workers to watch the NCAA Final Four on television, just two weeks after Denise's death. It felt good to laugh and enjoy the company of others; it also felt weird because she hadn't been dead that long.

My May 19, 1993, journal entry also tells of another example of the above: *Went to Jen F.'s house. We were joking about Denise. I felt bad.* The jokes were probably nothing, maybe teasing about things that had changed, but I still felt guilty for laughing at her expense. It's also laughter and joking that help us heal. Although it's difficult to keep that thought in mind sometimes, I know Denise wouldn't have wanted us to be overwhelmed with tears or mope through life.

Guilt occurs at other times, too. During the wake and funeral, I had cried so much that there were times I felt emotionless. People came up to me crying and all I could do was hug them. One girl, who had been on the cross country team with me and was a classmate of Denise's, approached me and told me she had once mentioned to Denise something about walking in front of a train. She started to cry. I told her it was okay, that it wasn't her fault. She felt a heaviness of guilt for telling Denise about something that she obviously didn't think Denise would ever do; I felt guilty for not crying at that moment. I now understand I couldn't cry because I had cried so much in the days between her death, the wake, and the funeral. My not crying, however, also allowed me to comfort others for a brief time.

Although I never felt much guilt about not preventing Denise's death, there are some events in my life that I regret. As a grade-schooler, I put masking tape on the floor to keep Denise from touching my half of our room. And I recall how she would tag along with my friends when I didn't want her around. It always seemed that we were a package deal. I couldn't understand why she didn't have her own friends.

When we got older and my life began to revolve around running, I started to alienate my family. I did and said a lot of things that I'm sure hurt them, Denise included. I do wish I had allowed Denise to be a bigger part of my life. However, I was very insistent on separating myself from her. That might go back to my childhood when we had to share so much and I wanted something that was my own. What I failed to see was that my sister looked up to me and just wanted to belong to something, too. My family almost never saw me run, by my choice. I always thought they would make me nervous and, again, I wanted separation. I remember the conference track and field meet my sophomore year in high school when Mom dropped me off for the meet. I almost suggested she and Denise stay to see me run, but I didn't and now I could kick myself. That night I finished third and ran the 1600-meter run in 5:29, my best ever. With Denise gone, I feel more regretful. That day, I had no idea she would only be alive for five more years.

Denise once told Mom that what started her on the road to bulimia was the oatmeal cookie dough she and I often made when I came home after track meets. In high school, I went through a period in which I was very obsessed with running and food, believing I had a weight problem. I'm saddened that I partly led Denise into that behavior. I didn't realize what an effect I had on her.

I don't think I ever told her I loved her. We used to talk about the difficulty of writing "Love" at the end of a letter before our names. I put "Always," and the last letter I received from her says, "Always." Wasn't Denise worthy of being told that I loved her? She wrote a letter to me once to tell me that she loved me; I never reciprocated.

I also didn't appreciate anything she gave me like the belt she got me the last Christmas she was alive. I had a cheap one that stretched so she bought me a really nice brand name one and I still wear it. The globe paperweight she gave me another Christmas is still on my desk. I wish I had said thank you more often. I will never idealize Denise like many people do with their deceased loved ones, only talking about the good parts of the person. I know she had her problems as we all do. I just wish I had shown more appreciation that she was my sister.

Although it was difficult to accept that Denise took her life, I knew many factors went into that decision, and they didn't include the tape I put on the floor. I get a sad feeling looking back at the things I did, knowing that I hurt her, but I realize it was all part of growing up, and I learned from those experiences. Unfortunately, many bereaved get caught in a spiral of guilt and have a hard time letting go of what they couldn't control.

Anger

What's not to be angry about? Our loved ones took their lives and didn't consult us. We feel helpless. It's hard to understand that they couldn't feel how we cared for them because they were so consumed with their own pain. It hurts that our lives are turned upside down, and we aren't sure how to turn them right side up again. When the denial and shock wear off, we might feel anger at that person for changing our lives and deciding they didn't want to be a part of our world anymore.

In the first chapter, I mentioned that calling Mom and walking through my parents' front door were two of the hardest situations I had to face after Denise died. No one had to inform me that life would never be the same again; the sinking feeling in my stomach told me loud and clear. After watching so many people cry at the funeral, including Dad, and seeing all the lives she touched, I couldn't help but yell at the casket. I wanted to pound on it; I wanted something to take that hurt away.

Anger might also arise from unresolved issues. Now that the loved one isn't here to work them out, we're forced to put the issues to rest on our own. If we don't work through those issues, they will fester and hinder the grief process. We must choose some positive ways to work them out; either by writing our loved one a letter, seeking counseling, or another expression of grief that works for us.

The level of anger from before the suicide also will impact our length of grief. The less anger in the relationship, the easier the road will be. That, however, is not typical for most people. There always seem to be unresolved issues to face after the death of a loved one.

What's more, it might be difficult to be angry with someone who is dead. Instead, we might focus that anger at a living family member. We want someone or something to blame and we don't want to accept that our loved one took his or her life. When we blame someone else, we are scapegoating. We also might feel angry toward ourselves if we fear blaming the person who died. Some bereaved are so hurt by losing the loved one that they would rather direct the anger toward themselves.

It's important to check to see if your anger is taking over your life or hurting the ones you love. Perhaps your anger is aimed at those alive. If it consumes you, it's wise to find a professional counselor to help you resolve any related issues.

Physical Symptoms

When we grieve, we ignore our physical health. Because we are bombarded with all these emotions, our bodies go into overdrive. Defense mechanisms are turned to full power. Grief also manifests itself physically as lethargy and illness.

As difficult as it appears to take care of ourselves (when all we can think about is the loss), no one can do it for us, and we can't grieve if we don't. We remember those first days after the death when we couldn't sleep or eat. If it weren't for the kindness of our neighbors who brought food to our house, we probably wouldn't have eaten. We didn't have to think about what to feed ourselves; casseroles simply appeared. Also, it's imperative we sleep and rest because there will be many trying days ahead, and we need all the energy possible to get through them. Some people might want to sleep all the time, feeling their energy slipping away from them as depression sets in. Part of this tiredness might stem from a lack of nutrients. We need to eat nutrient dense foods, assuring ourselves of optimum energy for the grieving process we have begun.

My energy level shifted after Denise died. The running theme through that time in my journal reads that I was "tired, eating a lot, and complaining." Looking back, I know I blamed the irritability and extra naps on the fact that I'd been working non-stop since January. I remember falling asleep at *The Daily News*. I just wanted to go home but I had to stay and work late nights. When I attended a sports journalism seminar at Churchill Downs in Kentucky a month after Denise's death, I overslept the morning of the seminar. The photographer who traveled with me called up from the hotel lobby where everyone was waiting. I couldn't get enough sleep. I napped more frequently, finding myself asleep most of the time when I was at my apartment. I'm sure it never crossed my mind that grief was getting to me and no around me knew much about grief either.

However, some survivors might not be able to sleep at all. They fear the dreams sleep will bring or having to wake up and relive the reality that the loved one is dead. If you suffer from insomnia, there are many healthy ways to help you sleep (listening to soft music, reading a book, and so forth). It's important to establish a regular bedtime and take the time to wind down.

When I went off to Colorado the summer following Denise's death, I blamed my fatigue on the altitude because Colorado Springs is at 6,000 feet and I normally lived barely above sea level. I expected it would take about a month to adjust to the mountain air. That didn't stop me, however, from setting high goals. I decided working out twice a day would give me more energy. I was wrestling with grief, adjusting to the altitude, and thought I could push myself twice as hard.

I began to wonder why my morning runs, although only three miles, were so difficult. Tim, a fellow intern, accompanied me a few times and, to my embarrassment, I had to stop and walk. My running journal reads that my legs were dead, the run was slow, or I was just tired. I even attempted a road race after living there only a month. I went out at a good pace but slowly died. My feet burned and my legs felt like lead. It was just like my daily runs.

Tim suggested I write down everything I ate for a day or two, and he would analyze it on the computer. I never did it. I just didn't want to. Sadly, neither of us had any idea of what was going on. I was agitated that I couldn't finish my entire run, and felt like I was eating too much. He only wanted to help. Exercise is very crucial to the grieving process because I might have struggled even more had I not been running at all. Running, even if I was walking some of it, allowed me time to reflect and think. It also helped me release some endorphins to lift my mood. I know it felt good to explore the streets of Colorado Springs. Many days I just wanted to go for a walk. I wanted to be out and feel the warm summer air. I needed to appreciate some of the good things I still had in life.

Not only was I tired and my metabolism altered, I also got sick more often. My resistance took a dive as a result of my grief. Early in college, I had developed some acne problems and started seeing a dermatologist. Even though my acne was treated with various antibiotics, a month after Denise died I developed a severe breakout.

"What's going on in your life?" my dermatologist asked at my next appointment. When I told him, he knew the stress had taken its toll. He told me his father had died by suicide so he was familiar with what grief could do.

If we don't take care of ourselves or allow ourselves to grieve, some of the physical problems that might arise include: sleeplessness, heart palpitations, irregular breathing, gastrointestinal difficulties, a choking sensation, weight loss, shingles, and chronic illness. That's just the top of the list. If we don't forge down the grief path, these difficulties will come back at least twofold one day when our bodies can't bear the grief any longer.

Consequently, we need to be gentler on our bodies than usual because the physical and emotional strain of grief is so high. Our needs include a solid amount of sleep, a good diet to keep our energy levels from depletion (eat smaller meals throughout the day if you have difficulty eating), exercise to lift our spirits, and the necessity to not abuse drugs and alcohol. Exercise, but don't overdo it. We know our bodies best and can recognize when to quit. Even a long walk will elevate the chemicals in the brain to help depression. Take each day one hour at a time if you have to. In basic terms, it's essential we take good care of ourselves and give ourselves time to heal.

Chapter Five
More Traveling on This Road Called Grief

Nothing stopped after Denise died. As we drove to her funeral, cars passed us en route to jobs or errands. When I'm in my own car and a funeral procession passes me, I think about how the lives of the grieving people are halted for that brief moment while the rest of us continue with our lives. I always thought the cruelest part of Denise's death was that the world didn't stop to acknowledge she was no longer with us.

While we trudge down the path of grief, we find our routines have been interrupted. All we want is to lie down and let the busy world go by, but we must continue to turn with the rest of the planet. We have to function, even when we don't think we have the strength to do so.

Also, we must move on with our lives although our loved one is no longer with us. Each day we do new things and experience life events without him or her. As we age and celebrate birthday after birthday, the deceased will stay as we last remember him or her. Although I have advanced through my twenties, my sister forever remains two weeks shy of her eighteenth birthday; she will always be that way, even when I am in my fifties. My husband, Joe, never met Denise, and, if we have children, they will never know their aunt.

A great wave of sadness overwhelmed me when Denise's friend Kristy had her first child, just over a year after Denise's death. Denise had been Kristy's maid of honor the summer before she died. Kristy said that when she learned she was pregnant (only months after Denise's death), she had an urge to call Denise and tell her the news because they had shared so much throughout their lives. Kristy called me the day Courtney was born and I went to the hospital to see her. I didn't expect it to be such a sad time for me, but as I sat in the hospital room with Kristy, her husband Terry, and other family members filtering in and out, someone was missing. Driving home, I sensed a large black cloud hanging over me. It was too hard without Denise. I wanted to be happy for Kristy with her new baby, not sad that my sister was gone.

Two years after Denise died, my brother Brian married. I expected his wedding day to be difficult. I thought we would be sad that Denise wasn't there. That wasn't the case, and I didn't feel sad when he and his wife, also named Denise, had their first child, Jordan. It was different somehow, probably because we had continued to move on with our lives without her.

Six years after Denise's death, my own wedding (for what would be my first marriage) drew near, and I wondered what it would be like minus her presence. I contemplated whether I would feel sad because she wasn't going to be there to celebrate it with me. As the day drew closer, I had many dreams in which she was at the ceremony although she was dead. I arranged for Mom and Joe's mom, Beverly, to light a candle for Denise and for Joe's brother, Andy, who was fatally stabbed in 1991. The anticipation was harder than the event. I sensed she was there with me in her own way.

We spent much of our childhood together dreaming, whether it was creating make-believe situations or planning our futures. Denise was a part of all the dreams I still cling to, and, as I look back, she knew them better than anyone else. She wasn't there when I finished my bachelor's, master's, or doctoral degrees nor will she be there when I will accomplish the rest of my goals. Life goes on without our loved one.

It's sad to us that we move on and fear we are forgetting him or her, but we have memories, something no one can take from us. When we realize we won't lose our memories of the person, we then begin letting go of the feelings and emotions affiliated with the death. It's much easier to release the loved one intellectually before emotionally. We never get over a death. Instead, the person always remains a part of us.

My mom sold the family home in 2011 and it was yet another aspect of leaving Denise behind, the only house Denise ever lived in. Each time we do something new, we let go of a piece of her because she isn't there to experience it with us. It's part of moving on. It doesn't mean we don't remember her, because we do think about her often. It just means we've adjusted to life without her.

While we organize our lives without the deceased, the death might set us on a different life path. Before Denise died, I worked hard at becoming a journalist and sports writing somehow fell into my lap, although I had previously pursued magazine writing. When Denise died and I found myself in a journalism internship at the Olympic Training Center, I started to rethink my plans. Because Denise had taken her life, I questioned much of what I wanted and believed.

Each of us lives by a paradigm representing a pattern of rules and regulations we live by. When a drastic change hits, our paradigm is destroyed and we must rebuild it. As with anything, when we reconstruct the paradigm, it's never the same. A death makes us wonder if this is the first of many bad things to happen to us, or if nothing bad will happen the rest of our lives.

That's the case when our lives are affected by death. We question much of it based on what happened. What do our lives mean when they ended theirs? When we lose a sibling to suicide, one factor we consider is how we aren't "supposed" to lose members of our own generation so early. We plan to grow old together. Why would we think any differently?

When my paradigm was ripped to shreds, I questioned journalism. As a beat writer for my college paper, coaches and players needed me to give them press and positive quotes. I wondered who talked to me because they simply wanted to talk and who might be "using" me. I always loved people and getting to know them and I knew when I asked them about events in their lives it was because I truly wanted to know, not because I was obligated. This was the curiosity, part of the writer in me, coming out.

Working in public relations in Colorado, I found myself on the other side of sports, working with some athletes and hanging out with others in the dining hall or around the complex. I dreaded returning to Ball State in the fall and covering football as a reporter; I would be back to my wondering game. By the time I left Colorado, I decided that after graduation I would enter a master's program and pursue a teaching license for health education.

I knew I was very lucky because a number of people supported me in everything I did and it was time I gave something back. I finally decided to accept my role as a positive influence and become a teacher and cross country coach. I envisioned all the great things I'd do in the classroom and change my students' lives. I also thought about telling Denise's story, hoping to help others.

One part, however, backfired. When we experience a death, it's advisable to put off any major life decisions that first year. Grief forces us to change, and we don't know what we will be like when we heal. We might make decisions to fill an empty space in our lives and think a change (such as a move to a new city) will work, or we want to escape the reality of the situation. We also might choose new paths because we think that's what others, or the deceased, would want us to do, but we need time to get our bearings and focus our energy on grieving before making changes.

When I began teaching, I realized I wasn't going to have the idealistic influence I thought I would have. I saw how I would be lucky to affect one life, let alone many. I didn't have the magic powers I believed I would possess when I walked into the room. I thought it would glow off me that Denise's death had affected my life in such a way that all the students would react positively to it. That didn't work, leaving me frustrated and unhappy.

I did feel confident that talking about Denise in class helped some students. Usually they were somewhat interested because she was real and I would pass around photos and a copy of her suicide note. I remember one class where a group of students gathered around the note trying to identify the song lyric she wrote at the end.

My need to become a writer, which had been with me most of my life, slowly resurfaced, leading me to where I am now, writing this book. I don't regret teaching or getting my master's degree, but now I'm continuing with my writing and trying to help others using Denise's story. Those big teaching dreams came during grief, but it would take more than a year for me to see what I really wanted and needed to do. People might argue that because I am in young adulthood, I'm in a time of transition and I could have driven down this road anyway. I don't believe that. Denise's death changed me in many ways I otherwise never would have known.

There is a much greater purpose in my life, but, unfortunately, I had to lose my sister to find out what that was. I had to grow, change, and trudge my way through grief to get here. I knew I wanted to help others in some capacity, and my writing initially served that purpose with a column I wrote about Denise in *The Daily News* (see "A Sister's Message…" following Chapter Nine). It wasn't until someone suggested I write this book, however, that I saw what I could accomplish with the written word.

These changes we endure don't only affect our purpose in life or our career plans. We also must consider relationships, especially romantic involvements. Some relationships we have will fare well while others will fall apart. Much depends on the connection before the death and how the survivor copes with the grief experience. It also rides on how well the other person in the relationship faces the loss. Everyone grieves differently. Death draws people together or, sadly, pulls them apart. It makes them stronger, or more vulnerable to future losses.

Even relationships that were thriving when the death occurred will be stressed because of the storm of emotions and grief. If two people can hold on and help each other through it, their partnership will endure one of the most difficult experiences in life.

The bereaved might discover that a partner can't cope with talking about the death. If this happens, the survivor feels isolated and the two people will drift apart. Suddenly there is something they can't share or that one doesn't want to share. On the flip side, the bereaved might not want to talk about the death, frustrating the partner who only wants to help but doesn't know how or when he or she is pushing too much. Again, the grief reactions rest on how healthy the relationship was before the death. The suicide bereaved is going to change to some extent after the death, and partners who can grow together will emerge stronger.

Those not involved in a relationship might seek out someone to fill the new empty space in their lives. They might look for someone exactly like the deceased, hoping for a "replacement," or they might search for someone just the opposite of the deceased to avoid all painful reminders of the loved one.

During that first year, I know I sought out some unhealthy relationships. Looking back, I can see how disastrous some of those situations could have been if they had continued. At the time, however, I couldn't look beyond what I was feeling. I wasn't trying to replace my sister so much as I was looking for an escape. I wanted someone to take my mind off what was happening in my life.

Some survivors initially draw closer to a partner, then pull away for fear of losing that person like they did the deceased. This depends on the survivor's past history of working through conflicts. The intensity of the loss also will be a factor.

I started to date someone seriously a little over a year after my sister had died. I didn't realize how much grief I still had to work through. I didn't know there was no time limit on grieving. While people would ask how I was doing, I felt that since a year had passed, I should have been okay. When I met this man, however, I found myself insisting that maybe things wouldn't work out between us. The reality was I wanted to pull away because I feared him leaving me as Denise had. I wanted to end this relationship on my own terms.

It's advisable that bereaved refrain from new romantic relationships through at least the first year of their grief, or until they have done the bulk of their grief work. The bereaved need to have some idea of who they are before getting involved with someone new. I don't regret that relationship, but I had no idea how difficult it would be at the time and why. Those fears dissipated over the years as I coped with my loss.

Most importantly, if we can grow and learn from the death, we will emerge as someone we never imagined we could be. Then we'll be ready for anything life hands us.

Do They Have Bad Days in Heaven?

Chapter Six

The Forgotten Mourners

After Denise died, finding information on sibling suicide survivors was difficult. I found plenty that would have been helpful if I had lost a spouse, child, or parent, but very little for siblings. And most of the sibling research didn't pertain to suicide. Each path of grief is different but I never found much of what to expect as a sibling survivor of suicide. What we do know, you will find in this chapter and the following one (on the family), although it's just the tip of the iceberg. We have a lot of uncharted territory ahead of us. Outside of general suicide bereaved's reactions, siblings have their own special set of feelings and obstacles.

Sibling survivors of suicide have often been called the "forgotten mourners," in part because there is little information available. Were researchers uncomfortable approaching the family in order to interview someone so young? It's easier for parents to want to protect children and adolescents from the pain or details of the death than expose what they might not be able to accept themselves. Very few research projects on older sibling bereaved have been pursued. I took part in two studies myself (one in Chicago on teenage deaths, one a dissertation in Colorado on the reactions of sibling survivors of suicide). In choosing to do both, I emphasized that I couldn't bring Denise back but maybe I could help others.

While more research has been done on sibling survivors of suicide, we still truly don't know how many exist. The best estimate can be derived from the U.S. Census Bureau, which states there are 1.85 children in the average family. By approximating one surviving sibling for each loved one that dies by suicide (48,000 per year) and that Judy Dunn (a developmental psychologist and author of *Brothers and Sisters*) estimates 80 percent of children in the United States and Europe grow up with siblings, then roughly 28,400 people become sibling survivors of suicide each year. Conservatively, in the last twenty-five years, over half a million Americans have become sibling survivors (710,000).

We do know that siblings usually must postpone their needs to help their parents through the death. They often become "double orphans" because they have lost their sibling and parents all at once. Suddenly, their support systems are gone. Sibling survivors might see their parents vulnerable for the first time in their lives. Siblings are told to be strong for their parents. Many siblings tend to think their needs don't matter because they must become caregivers. This is especially true for those who still live at home. They have to assume responsibility for taking care of the house and family if the parents are incapacitated from grief. Parents might rely on the surviving children to make them smile thus denying them a chance to grieve.

Sibling grief can be prolonged and complicated because siblings play an important role in the people we become. Suddenly the family is incomplete. We're forced to reorganize the roles within the family because we've lost a member. This is especially important if there were two siblings and one dies. If siblings are older and no longer live with their parents, they feel a sense of loss because they grew up together. As siblings are usually raised by the same two people and in the same environment, they understand each other very well throughout their entire lives.

The importance of sibling relationships can't be expressed enough. Chances are, the longest relationships in our lives will be with our siblings. This is because we are generally only a few years apart in age. We are supposed to grow old together. If we have spouses, we will be in early adulthood when we meet them; our parents are already much older than us.

It's with our siblings that we share the most experiences and memories. We don't choose or earn our sibling relationships. Rather, they are handed to us with the birth of the sibling. Because our sibling ties are so long, we witness more life changes with them than anyone else. As children, we spend more time with them than our parents. If we are close to them as children, that closeness typically extends into adulthood, or if we aren't close and have a jealous relationship with our sibling, it also will likely continue throughout life.

According to Victor G. Cicirelli, Ph.D., a sibling researcher and author of *Sibling Relationships Across the Life Span*, we share three other aspects with our siblings: genetics, a sense of family belonging, and a cultural heritage that we pass to our children. When our brother or sister dies, we lose a sense of family ties and security. Suddenly, an attachment to our family is gone.

Sibling relationships are not simple either. This is mostly because we share so much with them and we might see a lot of ourselves that we don't like in our siblings. As we enter our teen years, we sense a need to pull away from our siblings to develop our personalities independently. Once we become who we want to be, we can return and be close again, usually when we have families of our own.

Twin survivors of suicide must work through issues beyond those of a normal sibling relationship. They might not believe they have an opportunity to drift apart to create a personality on their own. Because many of them look the same, they go through life with a sense that they are never quite separated. In the same realm, they also have an emotional bond so strong that when one dies, the survivor experiences a phantom pain. This is similar to an amputee who feels like his or her leg is still there. The living twin hurts because a part of him or her has died and he or she can't accept it. Surviving twins might suffer a greater fear that, because they have such an identical genetic makeup, they will eventually die by suicide also.

Relationships among half or step siblings have their own issues related to the marriage of their parents. These siblings might not share as much history as full siblings. Instead, they have the difficulty of blending two families together. The mixing of families is never easy, although more prevalent now than in the past.

Our siblings are not supposed to die until we're old. Many of us make plans with them throughout our lives. We expect they'll be around as we get our careers into place, marry, have children, or achieve whatever is most important to us. During the last few years of Denise's life, the three of us sisters decided we wouldn't stand up in each other's weddings, a decision related to the hideous bridesmaid's dresses we'd seen. We thought it was more practical (and kinder) to give each other different roles in our weddings. Looking back, with Denise not here, it was a silly idea. I'm glad I didn't follow through with it and that I asked Karen to be my maid of honor. I wish Denise had been here for my wedding. It was difficult to read the card Karen gave me at my bridal shower, in which she talked about how she wished Denise were with us. Denise didn't get to wear the navy blue dress my friend Bonnie and I made for each bridesmaid. She didn't get to laugh at me on my wedding day, as I know she would have, when I put on my wedding dress. The family photo, our first since Brian's wedding in 1995, always will be missing someone. I believe it also was the last of any family photo we had because then my dad died in 2006 and my mom in 2014.

The sibling relationship remains an integral part of the people we become because we prepare for our societal roles with our brothers and sisters. Older siblings teach us what our parents might not have time to or want to do. Parents often ask the older siblings to help out with the younger ones. I know Mom asked this of Brian and Karen when Denise and I came along.

The sibling relationship can be classified into three specific ways: second parent, role model, and friend. My older sister is a good representation of the relationship in which one sibling acts as a second parent to the younger one. Karen was ten years older than Denise and told me she always felt like Denise's second mother. It was Karen who taught Denise how to use the toilet, with Raggedy Ann as the stand-in. She also took both of us trick-or-treating and played games with us, even when she had other things she would rather do. When Denise died, Karen felt that she had also lost a child. Karen's grief reactions, and of those who hold this relationship with their sibling, will parallel that of a parent's. Among these reactions is guilt for not preventing the suicide, or for not making the world a place in which the loved one wanted to live.

Flipping the ages around forms the second relationship. This is the role model relationship, in which the sibling who dies is several years older than the survivor. The survivor looked up to the deceased sibling as someone to emulate. When the sibling dies, the survivor feels very hurt because he or she doesn't understand how someone he or she role modeled could decide to die. The survivor might or might not have seen what was really going on in the deceased's life or what he or she struggled with daily. If surviving children weren't aware of any problems, maybe it was because the deceased knew the younger children looked up to him or her and didn't want them to see the reality of his or her difficulties. The survivors fear turning the same age as the deceased sibling, worried that they, too, will die by suicide.

Neither of these relationships describes the one I had with my sister. We were only three and a half years apart, more like friends. Siblings close in age are like twins in that they might experience the phantom pain, or loss of self, when one dies. In the journal Denise kept at the hospital following her first suicide attempt, she wrote that she was closest to me because of our ages. When Denise was born, Brian and Karen were both verging on adolescence, I wasn't even in school yet. Denise and I shared a room and played a multitude of made-up games. Because she was more like a friend and an integral part of my formative years, with her death I lost someone who influenced the molding of who I am today.

Denise was part of my creativity because she and I did a lot together. She took a lot of my childhood memories with her. There's no one to help me remember what happened at which Holiday Inn swimming pool we swam in during our family vacations. Denise knew more than anybody what I wanted out of life, whether it was aspiring to be a disc jockey or an Olympic runner. We were together so much that it was only natural she knew these things. In a friend-like relationship, siblings believe they have lost part of their identity and someone with whom they shared their lives. It's the same with our close friends who aren't part of our immediate families.

I admit things weren't always perfect. Denise and Karen frequently ganged up on me and made me the Monkey in the Middle. I was resentful of Denise sometimes because I had to share a room with her. We never hit each other, but we exchanged words and ignored each other for long stretches. Those rough times, however, are outweighed by happy memories. Part of growing up is learning how to communicate and get along with others and I learned this most from my relationship with Denise.

Gender of the siblings also plays a part in the grief cycle. Some brother-sister relationships are very close, almost in a "couple" sense. This brings a special set of difficulties as the surviving sibling copes with the loss of a confidant. Two brothers might have been close, not in that they spent a lot of time together, but because they held an emotional appreciation for each other.

When looking at sibling grief, we must consider the ages of the surviving siblings when they're faced with the loss.

Childhood

Many people think children don't grieve. They do, though their grief reactions differ from those of adults because they have undeveloped coping skills and very little understanding of death. They mourn only for short periods of time and return to their grief when they're ready. Their ages, as well as the response of their parents, influence them greatly.

If children are under two years old when their sibling dies by suicide, much of their reaction depends on their mother's response to the death. The sibling feels any change from the norm. Since a child's verbal skills are so limited at this time, the child expresses his or her feelings through crying, separation anxiety, and attachment difficulties.

Between the ages of two and five, children have a very egocentric view of the world. Their thinking is magical and they believe they have control over what happens. When a sibling dies, the children might think they made the death happen because of thoughts they had. The children also might believe they can make the dead sibling come back to life. This is compounded when the children are told their sibling "went to sleep." The siblings then fear that if they go to sleep, they might not wake up either. As they enter elementary school, children start to understand that death is permanent, but most still think it can be reversed. This is reinforced by cartoons in which the dead always return. By age nine, children begin to understand that death is part of life, a biological process that is inevitable. They also start to comprehend what the word "future" means.

It's difficult for children to understand how and why their sibling chose to take his or her life. Death is so removed from their experience that if their sibling dies, they fear they will die, too. They feel anger and abandonment, wanting to know why the sibling chose to leave. The children believe the future is gone because the sibling is dead. If no one allows the children to express their anger, it comes back years later manifesting as behavioral or physical problems. These include school or social difficulties.

Guilt plays into the children's feelings as, universal to childhood, we all wish our siblings dead at one point. It comes through anger and strong emotions after a fight or related situation. When the loved one actually dies, the surviving children are left to wonder if it was their fault because they wished for the sibling to die. Children will take the death personally because they can't understand that the sibling's decision was out of their control. The anger could also be directed at the parents for not protecting the sibling and keeping him or her alive.

They need the opportunity to attend the funeral (if they choose to), which provides a chance to say goodbye. By including children in the rituals and traditions that accompany the funeral, parents are helping their own grief, too. However, the children also might play "funeral" or "death." This is their way of acting out emotions and grieving. It's how they understand and let go of something so foreign to them.

Children will experience some of the physical symptoms of grief that adults endure. These include: stomach pains, depression, loss of appetite, and headaches. They feel physically hurt but can't express themselves emotionally until they're older and their coping skills mature. Any time children are grieving and develop physical or emotional difficulties, they should be examined, as these problems are probably related to their loss.

They need to talk about their feelings, especially because they face many challenges in the family, including the change of roles that will be explored further in the next chapter. It's a scary thought for many children that nothing will be the same again. They need to return to their routine and feel secure that life will go on. Children need to know someone will still listen and take care of them. Without anyone to hear them, they'll develop their own answers to their questions, leading to more fear.

Encourage those who have a difficult time talking to engage in non-verbal ways of expression. Examples include drawing, artwork, writing stories, and play (for younger children). After finishing, the child can be asked about what he or she created. It might lead him or her to talk about his or her feelings. The surviving sibling could also want to do something he or she had planned to do before the loved one died, such as putting a puzzle together.

Because of the stigma of suicide, many children are shielded from the details of the death. It's important that parents and adults are honest with children, even if they want to protect them. Children who are sibling survivors of suicide face the added burden of their parents wanting to guard them from the same fate. The children don't need to be smothered though. This could create clingy, immature children.

Sometimes people only remember the good about the deceased. They will talk about the person's good looks or great grades. The surviving siblings will hear this and think about the hospital stay or depression. The siblings will be confused because of the conflicting memories. However, other adults might only talk about what a hard time the deceased had. In this case, if the children remember the good times, they will feel the same type of confusion. What was real, what they saw or what the adult remembers? The survivors need reassurance that it's okay to remember the person as a whole, as we all have good and bad times in our lives.

Children need their parents at this time, but parents usually are too wrapped up in their own grief to give them enough attention. It's extremely important that parents take good care of themselves so they can be there for their surviving children who need to know, even though things have changed, they will be okay. If the parents don't cope, the chances are good that the children won't either. Parents need to continue with discipline. They can't let that go, in fear of losing another child, because when they emerge from their grief, they won't have the control over the children they once had. After all, children yearn for rules and discipline. When they have structure, they know they're loved.

School presents unique situations depending on the age of the children. If the nature of the death has been kept a secret from the children, they won't understand why teachers are whispering when they are nearby. If the suicide is known, other children might be uncomfortable talking to the survivors because their parents passed the stigma on to them. It's also possible that the parents created a new version of the sibling's death (such as it was an accident) to tell people outside the family, even when the children know it was a suicide. The children will be confused by this change of story. It's crucial to talk to teachers, counselors, and other school officials to make them aware of the situation. Many of those in the school setting don't know enough about suicide (or grief in general) to help survivors. If children's grades slip and parents and teachers aren't aware of grief reactions, they might attribute it to something other than the grieving process.

Classmates at school are placed in a difficult position because they won't know if the children want to talk about the death. They'll express sorrow and move on, while the surviving siblings, although asking that life go on as usual, will want to talk about what has happened. The survivors might feel they can't talk to their peers because the others won't understand. They might not have anyone willing to listen at home and hope their friends will make up for that.

A surviving sibling might think he or she is being tagged as "the kid whose brother killed himself." He or she will need help in overcoming that feeling. Parents of other children can prepare their children on how to help the sibling survivor by explaining that this is a difficult time and he or she needs a good friend.

Many reminders of the sibling could haunt the child if they were close in age. Teachers and friends might call the child by the sibling's name, or remind him or her of competition between the two. Reactions depend on the child's relationship with the deceased. Very jealous relationships are more difficult to overcome after suicide.

People don't realize that children who lose a sibling to suicide carry this through their lives. They'll always remember the sibling as he or she was before the death. Children will grieve for their sibling and want to honor him or her as they move on with their lives, forever altered by the loss. It's important to confirm their memories. Listed in the resource section of this book are wonderful workbooks to help children remember the one who died. There are also books included that help children understand they didn't cause the suicide.

Adolescence

When children reach adolescence, they face a wealth of physical and emotional changes so rapid that they don't know who they are when they look in the mirror. What they see one day is not what they see the next. Adolescents are adapting to bodily changes as well as finding their roles in society. They're most vulnerable to not coping well with the sibling loss because they're experiencing this transformation and already grieving the loss of their childhood.

They believe they're immortal because they can only think about one day at a time. We know the stories about the students who thought they could drive after becoming intoxicated or believed they could have unprotected intercourse and wouldn't get pregnant or contract a sexually transmitted disease. Death remains in a faraway place to them. Their death reactions are very intense because of this immortal thinking. Adolescents don't believe anyone they know will die either. They also don't face much death at this age. Typically, they'll lose a grandparent first. Suicide, however, along with accidental deaths and homicides, account for a high percentage of teen deaths, so when teens experience the loss of a sibling or friend, it's a sudden death.

Also, they're still trying to figure out what death is and what it means to them. Their anger could stem from trying to protect themselves from the loss. They might cry a lot, or not show any emotion at all. They are scared by the emotions they feel. If they have some knowledge of grief patterns, that can help them.

Adding all this together makes the adolescents' grief experience very difficult, and the death of a sibling means the survivors have lost a part of their identity, as well as a role model or companion. Although siblings are pulling away from their families as they prepare for adulthood, they're also looking for something to grasp on to. With a death, they might try to cling to what family is left because it now feels as if they are incomplete and "siblingless."

Familial role changes are especially difficult if survivors aren't sure what their new role in the family is. For many adolescents, their principle confidant is the mother. If she is overwhelmed with grief, the adolescents will suffer from losing that parental support. Again, siblings often "lose" their parents for some time forcing them to take over many roles in the family they're not equipped to handle. They must care for their parents when they're barely emotionally able to take care of themselves. The adolescents might stop grieving because they aren't sure if their feelings are "normal." They might not have anyone to turn to and tell them what they're feeling is okay. It's important to include them in all rituals of the death. This will help them cope.

Because the subject of the suicide could be considered off limits at home, the adolescents might feel more confusion. This was a key part of the 1984 television movie "Silence of the Heart" about suicide starring Chad Lowe. After his death, there is a scene where his surviving sister and parents are sitting at the dinner table and no one is talking. The sister tries to bring up the death but the parents don't want to discuss it. In real life, other siblings might not want to talk either and the surviving siblings could blame each other.

At school, the survivors are trying hard to fit in and be like everyone else, but when a sibling dies by suicide, it might be easier to deny feelings of grief just so they don't stand apart from the others. As adolescents taunt each other, those surviving a suicide will have to cope with their peers making remarks about the death. Others might be afraid to say anything about it at all. If adolescent sibling survivors don't have appropriate coping skills, they'll act out negatively (getting in trouble at school, abusing alcohol and drugs). They'll have a difficult time as they get older if they don't allow the grief process to run its course.

Surviving adolescents need a way to honor and identify with the one who died. This could be visiting a place the sibling who died never got to see or continuing activities they did together. They might choose to fulfill a goal their sibling never had the opportunity to do. As long as these motions don't become distorted (for example, the siblings start to take on the personality of the one who died), they're good ways for the surviving siblings to cope. A journal for teens who have suffered a loss is listed in the resource section of the book.

The adolescents who cope and grieve in a healthy way will find themselves stronger and with greater purpose in life. They will be more mature than most their age. Most importantly, they will take their sibling through life in a way that fits them best.

Young Adulthood

Young adulthood ranges from our early twenties to mid-forties. We continue to set our identities. We carve out careers and families of our own. We feel a great deal of hope because we have a multitude of goals we want to accomplish. As we leave high school or college, we think about pursuing a job in the career of our choice and/or beginning a family. We usually leave home at this time, looking to form ties that will become the basis for our own families. We try not to hurry along, but we feel the pressure to settle down with one person as we see some of our friends doing. The world is our oyster and we've left behind our teen years ready to take on life.

When Denise died I had just entered young adulthood, setting out to stake a life of my own, but I won't remember my early twenties this way. True, I had no secure adult patterns like most people in my age group. Instead, it will remain to me a time when my sister's death threw my planned course out the window. I was set to become a journalist. I really wanted to pursue magazine work, but the sports writing gig had fallen into my lap so I wasn't sure what would happen when I graduated a year later. I found myself floundering, becoming more and more disenchanted as the days went by and I continued to grieve for my sister. As I tried to establish my adult patterns, I had to start all over again. It put me behind where I wanted to be. I entered graduate school looking to find satisfaction in teaching.

If we lose a sibling during this period, we learn the hard way that life doesn't hold the unlimited promises we expected. It might not allow us all the time in the world to accomplish our dreams. We sense an urgency to fulfill what's really important to us. We could also feel guilt that we're going on without our sibling.

Suddenly, my sister decided she didn't want any part of our world. It made for a difficult time because only weeks after she died, I received my journalism internship and a scholarship award. All these positive things were happening even though her death was still fresh in my mind. In this time, I began to see I was headed down a road I disliked. I didn't want to be a sports reporter at a small-town newspaper. I cringed when I thought of doing it. I believed I could do something much greater, something that would satisfy a larger need in me than covering sports. It appeared that coaching and teaching would allow me that outlet, letting me become the positive role model I always denied I was before.

As a senior in high school in 1990, I handed in my captain's pin after the indoor track season. I didn't like being a vocal leader. I enjoyed the role of silent leader, leading by example and action. I was uncomfortable when people would approach me and tell me how I motivated them to run. That didn't sit well, especially when it came from my younger sister. After she died, I was ready to accept that responsibility.

Losing a sibling in young adulthood leaves us with a sense of vulnerability that life is more fragile than we ever thought possible. Just as it tells us that death affects us, it also brings death closer to our lives. We have a clearer feeling of it and because we're older, we're able to comprehend it better than we did in our adolescence.

When we enter our late twenties, we're faced with the reality that it might not be possible to accomplish all our goals. Our choices become more complex, especially if we have decided to settle down. Suddenly, there is a spouse we must take into consideration before choosing a new job or career move. We might have children and the large financial obligations that go along with them as well as with owning a house.

Our twenties will turn into our thirties. Those dreams from our twenties fade as we have accomplished other goals. We start to feel a real sense of our mortality. When we face the death of a sibling at this time, it makes us reevaluate what we believe in. If the death is a suicide, this hinders the grieving process even more and, as we get older, many of our co-workers and friends won't place much emphasis on the sibling loss. People forget what we share with our siblings. We don't live together anymore but we do share a lot of history with them. The adult sibling survivor must hunt for those special friends to talk and relate to about this loss.

Middle Adulthood

When we approach our mid-forties through our fifties, we want to slow down and enjoy what we have worked so hard for, whether that be a job and career and/ or family. It's a time when sacrifices become rewards. Our careers are going well and/or we are reaching the pinnacle of raising a family.

During this period, we are very stable, but the death of a sibling alters our course just as it would in young adulthood. The obstacle this time, however, is that it's much more difficult to make the changes we crave because we have a spouse and family that need to be supported. Additional responsibilities include career obligations.

We might be forced to question our definition of happiness as well as our purpose here on earth. Life seemed so smooth. It could be that we were questioning all this anyway as we tried to come to grips with the aging process. We'll feel time is passing too quickly. There's so much we want to do and so little time to do it. Do we believe in our definition of happiness? Did we accomplish what we really wanted out of life?

If a sibling dies during middle adulthood, there are some special issues to be considered. As friends and other family begin to die from deaths other than suicide, we start to lose our own generation, reminding us how precious our time is. Another important matter includes the deaths of our parents. There can be previous unresolved issues relating to a parental death, whether it is a disagreement of how their personal possessions were divided up or how the funeral was handled by one of the siblings. If this is the case and the sibling then dies by suicide, the guilt escalates.

We face the thought that we feel more obligated to our own families and parents than our siblings. That can bring about guilt that we weren't there for them when they really needed us. In fact, we could have been so absorbed in our own lives that we didn't notice how rough theirs had become. Even though we've lost a tie to our sibling, we might gain a stronger connection to their children, our nieces and nephews, to preserve what is gone.

Late Adulthood

Some researchers classify people between the ages of sixty and seventy-five as "young-old" and those over seventy-five as "old-old." No matter how they're classified, sibling suicide loss still affects them. Quite a few older people choose to die by suicide at this time because they're frustrated by their limited abilities. People in late adulthood face a loss of independence as many find they can't live on their own or even drive their cars. They could have a terminal illness and seek suicide as a means of ending their lives on their own terms.

Older adults do leave families behind though. Losing a sibling in late adulthood does one of two things: it intensifies the loneliness of the living siblings or it enhances the feeling that their time to die is coming, too. Siblings at this age usually have lost their parents and the sibling who dies by suicide might have been the only surviving member of their family, leaving a gap of memories when they die. Elderly people who know their time to die isn't far away won't be as motivated to grieve for the sibling. They know they're going to die soon, so they feel less reason to mourn the loss of a loved one. Much of this depends on their view of death. If they are ready to die, the emotions won't be as intense.

Relationships with surviving children and spouses factor in because there is communication with them, but if the elderly lose a sibling and their spouses have already died it only enhances the isolation. They might question their existence because they are the only ones left.

A sibling suicide death creates incredible changes for the survivors. While the deceased takes with him or her a lifetime of memories and a long-standing relationship, it forces the surviving siblings to rethink where they want to go.

Siblings either become prone to sickness and stagnation in their lives or are inspired to mature and find some way to enrich themselves. They become more sensitive to the needs of others and more alert to life around them. They reach out to the other siblings in the family, realizing they don't want to miss out on more than they already have, but some of this caring will result from the feeling that they could have prevented the death if they had been more concerned. Siblings will carry this into all areas of their lives.

Do They Have Bad Days in Heaven?

Chapter Seven
The Family Unit Copes

Denise's life became increasingly difficult in the early 1990s when she developed bulimia and depression. Being raped probably sent her over the edge. When Denise took her life, however, she exposed to society what we thought was wrong with our family. After all, society says something must be amiss with the family if one of its members decides not to live anymore. I know I felt it. I sensed people pointing at me from the front windows of their houses when I went on my daily runs. "Her sister is the one who walked in front of the train." Did I move away from Naperville because of Denise's death? Not consciously, as I had been planning to move away since seventh grade, but I'm sure there are people who do move because of the stigma. It's easier to start over where people don't know anything if we don't want them to, even though our problems follow us wherever we go.

We spend our entire lives trying to fit in. Society tells us we must be part of the group. I always wanted my family to be like others. For one reason or another, I thought we were just a little different. What I didn't know is that every family has issues, not only ours. Even the most outwardly "perfect" families in the neighborhood where I grew up were tangled with problems. I remember three divorces in families Mom told me she thought were "perfect." As someone once told me, if we think a family is "perfect," we don't know its members well enough.

Still, suicide exposes that something is wrong. And suddenly, we must contend with the family problems that might have led to this point. Fault lines in family relationships grow deeper with a suicide.

After the death, everything becomes exaggerated, or perhaps what had been lying beneath the surface is brought out for everyone to argue over. Not every family is the same so situations are different and each member of the family grieves differently. Even siblings won't grieve the same. Some will be mad, while it takes others years to feel the same pain. Because of this, family members must respect what the others are feeling at any given time and understand those emotions come later. Each person enters grief's different levels separately.

Some families refuse to bring up the suicide at all. Siblings wonder if they, too, will die by suicide (because they share the same genetic background) or what will keep them from taking their own lives. I've often contemplated how my parents had three children who desire to live but one who died by suicide.

Sometimes family members pull away from each other completely. They're trying to save themselves from guilt and blame and they think the best way is to retreat from the others. The siblings and/or parents might blame each other for the death. There are families where the siblings aren't on speaking terms after the suicide because they think the others caused the loved one to want to take his or her life. This is very difficult, no matter the ages of the siblings. If they're home, obviously there is tension as they try to grieve but spend most of that energy directing anger toward someone else. If they're older and away from home, it creates tension at family events.

Even sibling relationships that were good before the suicide become stressed. Some siblings use the opportunity to unleash all their anger at another sibling. They feel a freedom to open up their frustrations at the one they viewed as having the easiest life. The siblings might believe one in particular didn't understand what was going on at home or didn't spend enough time with the one who died. Suicide lowers the inhibitions of family members, making them more prone to expressing their feelings, even those that aren't valid. Suicide will change the entire fabric of the family. While sibling relationships are never static through life, especially during developmental times, a suicide will either bring a family closer or tear it apart.

Unfortunately, sometimes one surviving family member has to sever ties with the entire family (or certain family members) who don't want to cope, but it must be done so the survivor who wants to grieve and continue to live life can. If family members want to remain stagnant, they can't expect the others to as well. We must take care of ourselves because there's only so much we can do for others. We can't control what happens to us but we can manage how we respond.

Role changes affect the siblings. They either choose to take these new roles or are forced into them. For instance, who will take out the garbage? If the sibling who died played the protector for another who was picked on, who will guard him or her then? These are scary thoughts for a young sibling. Children lose a playmate. Older siblings lose a confidant. If the parents are aging, there is one less sibling to help with decisions about them. If the oldest dies, the next oldest thinks he or she must take over that role. As the youngest died in my family, I hated being the youngest alive. That wasn't my place. It aggravated me to think that my name would be after the "and" in the Christmas cards; that was Denise's spot. Mom tried to remedy the situation by telling me she would put Karen's dog,

Chaos, at the end.It's important, however, to be sure siblings have parts to play in the home. This could be as simple as helping make dinner or set the table. Those little things help them feel like a part of the healing because they're contributing. When the sibling is forced or chooses to take over roles that he or she is not mature enough to handle, it won't benefit anyone's grief process.

If only one sibling is left, he or she feels the burden of adding the loved one's role to his or her own. There is no one else to care for the parents when they get older and no other siblings to have grandchildren. When one sibling is left, all the roles from the deceased are given to the survivor. That's double of everything. However, some survivors feel relief when their sibling dies because they know they don't have to vie for their parents' attention or share their toys or mothers's jewelry anymore. They're thankful they don't have to fight over how to take care of their parents when they are older. For those who experienced an intense rivalry with their siblings, there is a feeling of "I won." Some of this relief related to winning could eventually manifest itself as guilt when the sibling survivors realize they didn't really win anything.

It's not only sibling relationships that change when there is a suicide though. The death of a child takes its toll on marriages, too. This obviously affects siblings no matter their ages. Couples grow closer or apart. It's difficult to grieve at the same pace. They must allow each other space without forgetting that their children don't need to be caught in the middle. It was a milestone the day Dad (who frequented the cemetery) asked Mom to go with him on what would have been Denise's twenty-second birthday. It was a small step, but to me, I hoped it meant they could find some common ground as they grieved the death of their youngest daughter.

Parents will try to protect their living children. They'll want to do more for them or give them extra gifts. They might not let them out of their sight. When I moved to Albuquerque, Dad kept saying that he and Mom were going to move to New Mexico. At the time, I was very annoyed because I was twenty-two years old, ready to start graduate school, and build my own life. Looking back, I know it was hard for them to leave me there. Denise had only been dead seventeen months and I was moving 1,000 miles away.

Many siblings will try to protect their parents, too. Some move home after the death of a sibling to take care of their parents. Others will shield their sadness from them, not wanting them to worry.

Siblings might try to protect their other surviving siblings from any hurt by burying long-held resentments. This obviously isn't healthy, but siblings are scared of losing anyone else in the family. I have become fearful of leaving my family. I hate saying goodbye to them when I leave town or they leave after visiting me. I worry that it will be the last time I see them.

In some families, the parents continually talk about the deceased child, making the surviving children feel as if they don't matter. The parents are so caught up in their grief, they appear to have forgotten they have living children. This goes back to what was said earlier about children losing their parents for some time after the death. It can lead to anger in the children who are alive when they feel deserted by their parents who have put the deceased child on a pedestal. They have other surviving children who need assurance that they're still loved. Those siblings want to move on. They miss their sibling but they want to continue with life.

Siblings perceive the family's problems differently than the parents. They might concentrate on any family difficulties that could have contributed to the suicide while the parents only think about the child who died. And the siblings sometimes believe they must make up for the parents' loss of one child by becoming overachievers, not realizing they aren't coping with their own grief.

Those siblings who marry and have children after their loss will be sad and possibly angry that the sibling who died isn't there to experience important events. Siblings who have children will worry that their own children will die by suicide. The family will be concerned about how other families view them or if one of the surviving siblings marries into a family with a suicide as well. Nothing is taken for granted after a sibling dies by suicide.

It's important for families to try to work together in the best way they can. No one grieves in the same form or space. Grief has no time table either. Each one of us will carry the loss through life in our own manner. By remembering and finding ways to talk about the loved one, each family can come to an understanding of the individual grief process. It'll be difficult for families, as they will lose connections with the person who died. Friends of the deceased pull away and no longer will important activities of the loved one (such as piano recitals or sporting events) be a part of the family. New connections and activities must be explored. This takes time, but it helps build the bridge through grief.

Chapter Eight
Is There Anything I Can Do?

Author's note: As a sibling survivor of suicide, you're faced with a wealth of unfamiliar experiences and emotions courtesy of the grieving process. Never before in your life has the need for the aid of friends, family, and counselors been so great. Everyone will desperately want to help you, but having never been this close to such intense grief before, they probably don't know how to go about it. This chapter is geared toward the friends, loved ones, and anyone else who wants to help a sibling survivor of suicide. If you yourself are a survivor, reading this chapter can help you understand their sometimes confusing reactions to your loss. If someone approaches you and asks, "Is there anything I can do?" give them this book and encourage them to read the following chapter.

I have a folder I created the summer after Denise died. It holds the cards and notes people gave me after my sister's suicide. Many friends chose to reach out then. Although I know a few people who closed themselves off from us, I treasure those who tried to help me and be there for me, even the ones I hadn't talked to since high school or didn't know very well at Ball State. I realize I am lucky to have such friends because they called me and continued to ask about Denise, even years after her death. It's nice to know they haven't forgotten.

They never judged us. They just listened. They let me tell the story of how I was feeling over and over, just as most suicide survivors need to talk to confirm their loss. The bereaved want to repeat the story, even when friends have heard it many times and think the survivor should move on. The bereaved don't expect those who hear them to have any answers. They just want them to listen. At the same time, it might be difficult for some bereaved to talk because they feel too much shame or guilt. When that happens, it's best for the friends to let the survivor know they're there if needed, and that they're willing to answer the phone at 3:00 a.m. Don't say you're available any time if you don't really want to be.

Let the bereaved know they aren't a bother. They might not want to let you know they crave help and suggest other people who need a listening ear more than they do. To draw them out, use statements like, "Tell me how you're doing today," or "You must be having a difficult time."

Here are some other suggestions:

1. Can you tell me about the death? That day?

What happened?

2. Tell me about the relationship with your sibling.

What was your sibling like?

3. Tell me what life has been like since he/she died.

Usually, the bereaved want to talk. They just need some encouragement because they might be afraid to bring up the suicide. If you don't mention it, they think you're ignoring it. The fear is compounded if someone had discouraged them from talking about the death. That happened to me. I began to believe I shouldn't talk about Denise and that there was something wrong with me for wanting to tell her story. I now realize the feelings were undeniable. I just picked the wrong person to talk to. Let the bereaved know you aren't sure how to help. You can't take the pain of the loss away but you can aid them in expressing it.

The bereaved need to repeatedly recite the details of the suicide. However, survivors won't know how upset others become by this because all they're thinking about is seeking an answer to "Why?" And they're hoping each time they tell the story, it'll bring clues to light. I don't know how many times I've told the story of my sister's life and death. To this day, I still feel better telling it because it brings about some peace in me. Each time I repeat the story, I let go of Denise's suicide a little bit more.

Don't underestimate the power of hugging or allowing them to cry. Sometimes they don't need someone to talk to, they want someone to let them cry and give them a hug instead. Children and adolescents yearn for this, too. Some people never outwardly say that's what they want, so allow them your shoulder to cry on or your arms to hold them, no questions asked.

Other ways people helped included my sister Karen sending me a book about grief called *How to Survive the Loss of a Love* by Melba Colgrove, Harold H. Bloomfield, and Peter McWilliams. It was something I could read at my leisure and help me manage. Alan Wolfelt has a series of books called *Healing Your Grieving Heart: 100 Practical Ideas* for all ages. Each book has pages of ways to help cope with a loss (see the reference section of this book for more information). My friend Jen D. made me a tape of great songs. Knowing she took the time to create something for me made it very meaningful.

A few weeks after Denise's death, I ran into a girl I knew from the cross country team on campus. I hadn't seen much of her that spring because I was covering men's basketball. We stopped to talk for a moment, but she told me she was having contact lens problems so we continued on our separate ways. Shortly after, a "letter" I wrote to Denise was published in *The Daily News*. (See "A Sister's Message…" following Chapter Nine.) This same girl wrote me a note to tell me how sorry she was because she had been complaining about her eye problems and had no idea my sister had just died.

After about three months, society says we should be okay so people stop sending cards or letters, but this is really when survivors need them the most. Although society says survivors should feel fine, most of us don't. Support is crucial at this time because the shock has recently worn off, and three months isn't long enough to reorganize one's life or cope with the loss.

While many people were there for me in those first months after Denise's death, I truly appreciate those who continued to support me even years later. I developed new friendships because of Denise's death while others drifted away when the friends couldn't handle talking about the suicide.

That first summer, there were days when those waves of grief crept over me and, because the grief experience was so new, I didn't know what was happening. Other days I woke up feeling terrible that my happy dream wasn't reality.

The June 30, 1993, entry of my journal tells of such an experience: *I felt horrid when I woke up today, but I talked to Kurt (one of my co-workers) and gradually through the day, I felt better.*

When someone listened, it always helped. The bereaved just need to talk and talk and let out their feelings.

I made one friend in Colorado who was a great source of support in the second half of that summer. How I told Phil about Denise, I don't know. I do remember that he offered me his car if I needed to get away and, one night when he was out, he left his room open for me so I could have a bit of privacy from my roommates if I wanted. We talked some about Denise, but he was there to give me the support (as well as space) I craved.

I am still grateful to people who remember Denise. Even almost a decade after her death, I like to recall the things we did and want to know what others remember about her. It's hard, however, to find people who want to talk about the past. Sometimes, it feels as if many people have put her behind them and don't want to be reminded of what was. Years later, please ask the surviving sibling about the one who died or bring up a funny or happy memory. Sibling survivors want to know others still remember the jokes their loved one told or the times spent with them. With mutual listening, we can help each other through our grief.

When bereaved don't want to talk, encourage them to pursue another outlet for their emotions. They might be so angry that they don't know how to express it. Creative expression like artwork or writing might work well. They don't have to share it with you, although you can try and draw them out by asking about the project. Don't force them to share their feelings, be gentle and perhaps they will in time. There is also a wonderful compact disc called *Before Their Time*, a compilation of songs about loss that could help survivors articulate their grief if they heard a song they could relate to. Loss journals to remember the loved one are available, too. They include *I Remember…I Remember: A Keepsake Journal* by Enid Samuel Traisman (listed in the reference section of this book).

Another way to help the bereaved express his or her feelings is by encouraging him or her to write a letter. Then the bereaved can go to the grave and read the letter to the loved one. At this point, he or she could take someone with him or her so he or she can discuss the letter. Again, don't force him or her to do this because it might be very private. Ask kindly and don't be offended if he or she tells you he or she would rather go alone.

Also, remember men and women grieve differently. While women typically prefer to talk and express their emotions, men generally rely on action. This is why most support groups are made up of women (and because more men than women die by suicide). Men might choose some sort of physical activity (running, lifting weights, etc.) to cope. I know of one father who, after losing his son in an accident, made wreaths of wild grapevines during the holidays. Men also like problem-solving activities. They might get involved in fundraising for suicide prevention or related causes. However, it's not always that black and white– while gender does play into how we grieve, one can't assume that just because someone is a male or a female that he or she will grieve one way or another. While one could say that personality might be a better descriptor of how one might grieve, one can never completely predict what we will feel and do when a loved one dies by suicide,

Space is another important aspect of grief for the bereaved. Sometimes being with others can be overwhelming when coping with grief. There's a need to be alone at times. I took long walks some nights while I was living in Colorado. I had to get away from that part of my life and just be out in the open. One night I even walked to a park and sat on the swings awhile. And while some survivors will crave space, others fear it. Then some, like me, choose to split their time between personal space and spending time with others.

I returned to Ball State a different person. I continued to change, even if I didn't want to. And I wasn't "over" Denise's death like some people hoped. Who could I turn to then? Support groups and counseling are viable options for survivors. I will touch more on both in the next chapter.

Because I was unhappy with the counselor I was referred to and didn't have access to a support group, I turned to the priest at my church. When I returned to Ball State the fall after Denise's death, I began to spend some time with Father Dave at the recommendation of Sister Rita, who had driven me home after Denise died. I arranged to meet him between my day classes and evening newspaper work. He let me talk, whatever it was that I wanted to discuss.

My instructors at Ball State were wonderful, too. One invited me to spend the weekend at her house when I needed to get away while another gave me information on a grief group at her church. And there was Pat who had "adopted" me one day in church the previous year. She picked me up almost every Sunday for Mass and invited me over for dinner many times. My January 30, 1993, entry mentions her: *Pat and I had a really good talk. I needed to just talk and talk about Denise and her death. Thanks Pat. I need to thank her.*

As we wound through an entire year without Denise, we also encountered holidays without her for the first time. Her birthday was only two weeks after she died and, at that time, people still called and wrote because the death was so fresh. For some, this isn't true because the birthday might be six months after the death. Then there are anniversaries and birthdays of other family members.

Thanksgiving and the holiday season that followed were the most challenging for us. By then, everyone had gone on with their lives and expected us to do the same. This, however, wasn't the case. It was hard because I wanted others to acknowledge what had happened, but it seemed like no one would. When trying to help the bereaved, these are key times when they need to hear from someone. They want to know someone is thinking about them on these difficult days. The survivors aren't sure what to expect at this time and it helps tremendously to hear from people. Any meaningful days in the bereaved's relationship with the loved one will be
difficult.

Another important day they need to hear from those who care is the anniversary of the death. They want to know people are thinking of them and the significance of this day. They need to know others haven't forgotten. The first anniversary is usually the hardest for bereaved. If they haven't allowed grief to run its course, however, then subsequent anniversaries could prove to be more difficult.

As the first anniversary of Denise's death approached in March 1994, my roommate Andrea mentioned that she wasn't sure what to do because the anniversary had been on her mind as well as mine. It made me feel good that she was thinking about how to handle it, even though she had never been in such a situation before. She also hadn't known me when Denise died. The following year (1995), when I was in Albuquerque for the second anniversary of Denise's death, she sent me a card to let me know she was thinking about me. Nothing could be more appreciated.

It's significant when someone does something more than send a card after the funeral. In the days immediately following the death, the bereaved might not be able to get through each day and do all the things usually taken for granted. For instance, our society has a habit of taking food to the mourners' homes. It's not only to be nice but also so the family doesn't have to cook or think about what to eat. So much food was delivered to my parents' house that they invited everyone over after the funeral because there was no way we could possibly consume it all. As I mentioned in the first chapter, a woman we didn't know dropped off a bag of paper plates, napkins, and eating utensils. How thoughtful, because then we didn't have to do dishes. Who could even think about doing dishes, anyway? The opportunities for helping during those first days are endless: answering the phone, calling people who need to be informed of the death, and folding the clothes that have been sitting on top of the dryer since the suicide. However, I have also heard of people who crossed the line and made the funeral arrangements for the family. Please ask the family what is appropriate for you to take care of for them.

This extends into the weeks and months after the death. Grief doesn't just happen over one day and then disappears. It's a long process for the family to endure and not enough to offer to help the bereaved. Go over to the house with a mop and bucket and clean the floors. Take the dog for a walk. Do the grocery shopping. Take your friend to the movies or shopping for the afternoon. Friends know what friends like most, and if it means showing up with a new quilt pattern to work on, then go ahead.

It's important to be aware of what you shouldn't say to the bereaved. Because we don't talk about death or suicide in our society, survivors are in an awkward situation because many people are afraid to say anything, or what they do say hurts the survivor. People mean well but it doesn't always come out that way.

Even if you don't know what to say, tell them you're sorry and offer to be there for them. Let them know you're thinking about them and their loss.

In the brief time after the death and beyond, there are comments people make when they try to help. They include, "I understand." Unless they've been through a suicide, they don't. They say this because they think they do, but it only results in the survivor's defense mechanism kicking in. People also say, "Time heals all wounds." It's true to an extent but the survivor needs to grieve and not be reminded of the cliché. Another popular one is "you'll get over it." Unless people have been through a death, they don't realize we never get over it. Instead, we learn to cope and integrate it into our lives.

What the bereaved need following the suicide death of a sibling isn't hard to give. More than anything, it just takes a little thought and time. They need the opportunity to talk, if that's what will help. The suicide bereaved want people who aren't going to judge them for what they're going through or what their sibling chose to do. They have no control over the grief experience and need to allow it to run its course.

As the months go by following the death, the phone calls, visits, and cards become even more important. This is when most people forget and society says it's time to go on. Give them more support then. All it takes is a phone call or card to say, "I'm thinking about you. How are you doing?"

Lastly, it's going to be the special days the bereaved shared with the deceased when they especially need to know others haven't forgotten them or their loved one. The suicide bereaved want to know that while others' lives have gone on, they haven't been left behind.

Do They Have Bad Days in Heaven?

Chapter Nine
How Will I Ever Survive This?

When you're faced with the suicide loss of a sibling, please keep in mind that now, more than ever, you'll need to take good care of yourself. Unfortunately, no one can do this for you. Your life is never going to be the same, and it might take time for you to adjust to this. This means both physical and emotional stress will tax your body. Make sure you take the time to sleep during this sadness, even when you only want to stare at walls or stay up all night searching for answers.

You'll also need to eat well. Because your body is enduring so much, more energy than usual is crucial to get through each day. As a tradition in our society, many people will bring food to you immediately after the death so you don't have to cook. This might be the only way they can show their sadness, but it's wonderful because it means one less worry for you and/or your family. The kindness of strangers is amazing.

Your body doesn't only need sleep and nourishment; it also needs relaxation. With so many emotions ravaging you, a good workout, whether it be walking or running or just screaming on the top of your lungs (like someone told me she did once) will help release your emotions. I ran all through my grief, even when I had to stop and cry. My body dragged during the summer in Colorado, partly from the altitude, but mostly because of the stress on my body. I walked some days, having run so far, there was no way I could make it home. It bothered me, but the time away and just enjoying the bright sunshine helped me immensely.

Keep your workload light. You won't be able to do all you did before your grief journey began. In time, your energy and concentration will return. And remember to laugh! You will enjoy life again. Do the little things that make you feel good. Your loved one doesn't want you to suffer because he or she is gone.

Allow yourself time to be sad and let the emotions flow. Set aside a block of time during the day to think about your loved one. It could be ten minutes or three hours, perhaps at the end of the day when you get home from work. This allows you to gain some control over what looks overwhelming. You might feel very wiped out, but you're slowly letting your body heal from the trauma it has suffered. It's not going to be easy; I know that from my own experience. If you let it out now, however, it means you will hurt less later. A wound that isn't treated will fester and become infected, but if it is cleaned it will start to heal, just as we will in grief if we allow ourselves to meet it head on.

You have many options to let go of emotions besides crying, especially because you might reach a point where you are all cried out or feel you need to do something stronger. Not long after Denise died, I started a letter to her that I shared in Chapter Two. It talked about basic parts in my life, just as if she were away on a trip. I wrote everything I wanted to share with her. Some people need to write a letter to ask all their questions or to let go of any hurt or anger they feel toward the deceased.

Many people prefer to write one long letter with all their feelings, but I wanted to do mine on separate days because I felt different emotions and experienced events that brought back memories of my sister.

I also started a page with songs that reminded me of Denise and memories of things we had done together. I included "Harper Valley PTA" because we listened to it on our little record player and Pat Benatar's "Shadows of the Night" which we used to roller skate to in the basement (neither song has any lyrical significance other than we liked the way both sounded). Then there's Garth Brook's "Rodeo" which she sang for a speech on the history of the sport only months before she died. The taped speech is the only video we have of Denise. This list of songs doesn't mean anything to anyone else, but it confirms my memories on paper. If you don't want to write the memories on paper, make voice recordings to play at a later time.

Some people choose to take the letter to the grave and read it to the loved one, giving them a sense that the person "hears" it. You can take someone with you, if you feel comfortable, and then you can talk about the letter when you're done reading. A journal is another great way to help you emotionally let go. I've kept a daily journal since seventh grade, and it became especially important after Denise's death. I don't use it to record all my feelings like some people do, but I do write down my daily events and, when I need to, my feelings. Many people find it useful to have a place to write all those emotions down. It's also a great reward to look back later and see how far you've come. I can do that today, seeing the progress I've made over the years.

A book called *I Remember…I Remember: A Keepsake Journal* by Enid Samuel Traisman is available for those seeking a place to put feelings about the loved one and his or her death. Alan Wolfelt also has a series books called *Healing Your Grieving Heart: 100 Practical Ideas*. (Please see the reference section for more information on the above works.)

You might find that you express yourself best through some sort of artwork. Paint a picture or mold some clay. As long as the means of expression are positive, it's a great way to cope. Or music. A compact disc of memorial songs and music called *Before Their Time* is available. We often find comfort in lyrics and music when we locate ones that express how we feel.

One of the most important parts of grief is talking. You'll want to recite the details of the suicide over and over, not even aware that those around you don't want to hear them again. You'll do this because you're searching for an answer to the "Why?" question. You hope that each time you tell the story, you'll find a clue. I still feel better talking about Denise's life and death today because it's the best way I can let go of her suicide.

Seek out your friends, but remember there comes a time when you might wear them out. Don't feel discouraged if they have a hard time listening after a while. Put yourself in their shoes and see they're trying to help you with something that's probably very distant from them. And if they knew the deceased, they're also wrestling with their own grief. Kristy is one friend of Denise's I always knew I could call if I was feeling down. She misses Denise in the same sense that I do, as someone with whom we shared our lives. Through mutual listening, we helped each other cope with the loss. I know I called her at least once from Colorado and have occasionally since then. It always feels good to talk about my sister. People told me that if I wanted to talk, they would be there. I took some up on it, not knowing how comfortable they really were. If they offer, it's worth it to call them. They want to be there for you, and think they're helping you if you let them. They can't stop the feelings of loss but they can help you express the pain and cope with it.

Your co-workers and friends might not know what to say to you either. Although you can't understand why they don't approach you about the suicide, it really might be that they aren't sure what to say or how you'll react. They might be relieved if you don't want to talk about it, because then they don't have to offer help. To avoid a difficult situation, they believe it's best to ignore the death or distract you. It will be up to you to tell them what you need. I try to remind myself of this because there are many times when others aren't sure what to say. They're uncomfortable asking how Denise died. I'm not ashamed to tell them about her suicide, but death in our society is such a touchy subject that it's no wonder people aren't sure how to react. I once read that death has replaced sex as the one topic we can't talk about.

We are the bereaved on the inside of this bubble looking out, wanting people to talk about what happened. The bereaveds' lives are changed forever and we want to restore as much normalcy as we can. When we don't hear from people, it hurts because life keeps changing and we can't control it. On the other side, they are on the outside looking in, not sure what to say to us because they haven't experienced a death, especially a suicide. They aren't sure what they can ask or talk about.

You don't owe anyone an explanation for your behavior, your crying, or your not wanting to talk at all. There are times that you decide not to talk about what's going on in your life and that's okay. Your life is not an open book and you can share it with those you choose. You probably can't completely reveal to others all that you're feeling anyway, knowing they could never understand. It's up to you.

If you don't have friends you feel comfortable with, or you believe there are issues you need to work on, turn to a support group and/or a counselor. A support group for survivors of suicide loss allows you to talk with those who understand and have walked a parallel path. This is a group of people who are non-judgmental and have been through similar circumstances. They know the pain you feel or they wouldn't have turned to the group themselves. This is a place where you might connect with others willing to meet with you on your own time to talk more in-depth about what you've been through. You'll see from the others in the support group that life will be okay. You will make it. Suicide bereaved also band together through support groups to work on suicide prevention projects. The suicide bereaved want to keep as many people as possible from experiencing the same pain they have. These groups might meet on person or online virtually.

Some siblings just need someone to talk to with whom they can relate. Siblings want to be with people who have had a similar experience. When my sister died, there was very little access and information for the siblings of suicide loss. That's greatly changed as many siblings have banded together to form sibling groups both in person and virtually.

I met a woman at a support group who told me she wanted one for siblings because her experience was so different than her mother's. It's difficult to attend the same support group as your parents. They perceive events differently or you think you have to protect them from hurting further by not talking (this also works the other way around). At support groups, however, one sees that he or she is not isolated and life will eventually be okay.

I don't know if there was a suicide bereaved group in Muncie, where Ball State is located. My guess is that I didn't look as I couldn't have attended the meetings because I had classes and worked at the paper five nights a week.

I ended up trying some counseling, arranged for me through my church. But I only went once as evidenced in the September 16, 1993, entry of my journal: *I'm not going back. She was nice, but I felt like she was putting words in my mouth and made my life out to be worse than it is.*

I wish counseling had worked for me, but some mental health professionals choose not to work with the bereaved or simply aren't trained to help them. Unfortunately, the suicide stigma can extend into counseling as well. For some bereaved, especially those with complicated grief, professional help is essential. Shop around for a counselor and ask for referrals from people you know. There are a lot of wonderful, caring counselors willing to work with you and help you heal.

Seeking counseling or therapy is a good idea if you feel overwhelmed with emotions, such as guilt or anger, because those can bleed into other areas of your life. The counselor must be someone who stands on neutral ground and/or sees your issues in a new light.

You might need therapy if you have a history of mental illness in your personal life, addiction problems, you were very close to the sibling who died, and/or you witnessed the suicide/found the body. Make sure you're coping with all the issues in your life, whether or not the above applies to you. It's important to cut right through grief so it doesn't come back to you later in a more complicated way.

If people tell you that you "aren't supposed to" still feel badly, keep your chin up. Listen to your heart because you know yourself best. If it's breaking, you can't ignore it just as you can't leave the dish that fell off the counter and broke on the kitchen floor.

In time, you won't feel a pressing need to tell people what happened as you do in the beginning. There were many instances when I wanted to blurt out everything about Denise. No right or wrong answer exists on how many siblings to tell people you have. I can't deny Denise was ever in my life so I say I have a living older brother and sister as well as a younger sister who died. Yes, people ask what happened to her but I don't mind talking about her because it usually comes into the conversation when I talk about this book anyway. She's still a part of my life, but some people choose not to mention a deceased sibling at all. It depends on whether or not you're willing to chance what questions it might lead to.

In addition, there's no hurry to clean out your loved one's personal belongings. They aren't going anywhere, nor do you need to rid your house of them. If you're feeling angry, you might throw everything out and be sorry later, but it's not wise to make the room into a shrine either. Pack everything into boxes until you're ready to sort through them. We sorted through Denise's room a little at a time and it worked well. Each time I was home, we cleaned out more, as much as our emotions could handle, and then stopped. It doesn't matter what others do, however, you need to do what works best for you.

It's harder for siblings in this area if the bereaved are much younger. They most likely won't get a choice in what is kept because the parents will make all the decisions. And if they are older, the sibling's immediate family (spouse, children) will do the same. Siblings should be allowed to keep some items of significance if they want them. It's nice to have a piece of our loved one near. I have a little owl from McDonald's on my desk that Denise got on a trip we took with Mom to Denver. He's from a Disney movie. I sometimes wear her first communion cross and her class ring on a chain. I have some of the things I gave her as gifts that I got back. I keep them out because it's like having a little part of her with me.

After losing someone to suicide, there are many things we wish we had done or said. As mentioned before, sometimes writing those down can help. We might find things we wish we had done with the loved one or bought for him or her. Now that we can't, there's a sense of remorse that we missed our opportunity. This situation is especially true with siblings because relationships can be so close that we shared a friendship with our loved one as well. There are many things we can go ahead and do, even if that person isn't with us. This includes visiting places they never made it to or attending events we were supposed to go to together. It might be hard and take a long time, but if it's important to you, then you'll want to go ahead and do it.

The bereaved want to pay tribute to their sibling or memorialize them in some way. Obvious ways are memorials purchased either on Web sites or through support groups. When working the 1996 Olympics in Atlanta, an event Denise would have attended had she been alive, I bought a brick at Centennial Park with her name and the years she lived. I was overwhelmed with emotion when I filled out the paperwork. Two people visited the site after it was placed in the park, found it, and took photos for me before I got there myself. Other bereaved choose to name scholarships after their loved one. It depends on our means and what feels right. While there are many ways to remember your loved one online today, for many years we participated in the "Faces of Suicide" quilts where each block represents one person who died by suicide. These quilts traveled to events, much like the AIDS quilts, to give a "face" to those who have died by suicide.

Then there's the cemetery. Someone asked me whether I went to the cemetery because I felt my parents wanted me to or if I really wanted to go there. I've never gone because I felt forced to be there. I remember one time, feeling so frustrated that I made the twenty-minute drive just so I could sit and talk to Denise, who was no longer alive, to listen to my problems. Going to the cemetery allows the reality of the loss to set in on all levels, not just intellectually.

Some people say only the person's body is buried there, and their spirit is somewhere else so they choose not to go. In our society, it's traditional that we visit the cemetery, out of respect for the deceased. It's not a problem if you don't want to go, only if you can't accept the death and refuse to even drive by the cemetery and admit your loved one is buried there.

It might help to take other people to the cemetery, whether it's because you want someone there when you read the letter you wrote to the deceased, or just to have someone to talk to.

I sometimes pick up a rock from a river in New Mexico and place it on her grave when I visit Chicago. I try to take rocks from places she never visited. That comforts me. Other people leave flowers. There's something each of us can do to ease the ache inside us.

When it comes to anniversaries, birthdays, and holidays, the anticipation will always be worse than the day itself. There are no set guidelines for what to do on those days. I know people who go out and celebrate the person's life on his or her birthday and others who let the day go by and don't think about it at all. I try to acknowledge the day somehow, but as the months draw closer to March and the anniversary of her death, I'm filled with feelings of what was going on during the last weeks of her life. I remember the trip to Nashville Karen and I took a month before Denise's death, then going home the day before the basketball game and that being the last night with Denise. No matter what we do, these feelings change each year.

The following March after her suicide, I took a spring break trip to Colorado and had a great time. Part of me felt like I was going home, even with all the sadness I endured while I lived there the previous summer. Back in Indiana, I was out for a walk with Father Dave. I believe it was right around March 18 and I was telling him I felt great. It didn't even bother me. It hit the next week. Somewhat belated, but it still got me. I felt a wave sweep over me as I emotionally acknowledged the anniversary.

I've always thought about taking that day off and somehow honoring Denise, but I haven't come up with something I'd really like to do yet. I try to find some time on that day to remind myself of her, but I hope to one year do something bigger. I don't know, perhaps a long bike ride or a hike in the mountains.

For the two-year mark of Denise's death, my parents drove to Albuquerque. They arrived as the track meet I was coaching at ended. We didn't do anything special because we don't have to. She's on our minds and we acknowledge her in our own ways. Birthdays are the same although I don't mark her birthday on my calendar anymore. That felt strange the first few years. She'll always be seventeen. She doesn't age with the rest of us.

Holidays, anniversaries, and birthdays will be different. Traditions change while others stay the same. Again, do what makes you feel most comfortable. Do it because you want to, not because others say you have to. Having a plan often helps

A loss, such as a suicide, can cause a person to do one of two things; either move forward in inspiration or set back into sickness and stagnation. My hope for you is that you feel inspired by your loss and make positive changes in your life and find ways to honor your loved one's memory. If you do experience continued sickness and stagnation, then please seek counseling.

Some bereaved go on to help others. That's great, but be sure you cope with your loss before you aid those in fresh grief. If you don't help yourself first, you'll find you can't cope with their problems or that you are using them for your own grief work. After trudging through your grief, you'll be a great help to those first experiencing it. They'll appreciate having someone to talk to who has been there and know they can express their feelings without judgment.

There are many other ways to be inspired by a loved one's death. They might include carrying out some life work of the deceased. Think of those things that were important to your loved one. We planted trees in a national forest in Denise's name. She loved older people and had a great respect for our military veterans so those are examples people we can help in her memory.

It also could be through helping causes related to bulimia, rape, depression, and suicide, as I have done. I wouldn't have written this book without Denise's suicide. If I could bring her back I would, but I can't, so I need to help others to ensure that her life and death aren't forgotten. I can aid others through what she taught us.

When coping with grief, there's no other way to work it out than to go right through it. Facing grief is the best defense you have. It'll be hard and you'll want to give up. I cried many times, and when I was done crying, I was tired and didn't want to climb another hurdle. But when I look back, I see how far I've come and how glad I am that I chose to work through what I was feeling so it didn't haunt me later. Grief is a very active process. You can't let it go by passively. You need to attack it.

Plodding through grief means redefining your life so you find meaning in it once again. You won't be the same person you were before you lost your sibling to suicide. You might question much of your life such as your values and definition of happiness and success. I know because I was there. But life will be okay. You'll accept the loss and you won't forget your sibling. Your brother or sister will always live in your memories or wherever you choose to honor him or her. In time, you'll find a new sense of purpose. Don't expect it right away. I didn't know I was going to write this book until two years after Denise died. You'll know what it is you're supposed to do when it's time.

Reading my journals, I can't believe how far I have come. I remember so little of those daily feelings. A few years after Denise died, I talked to Tim, who had been an intern in Colorado with me, and he commented how he had had such a good time there. Then he clarified what a difficult period it had been for me. I had been thinking about that myself and gave him an answer I don't think he, or I, expected.

"I don't remember the bad times," I told him. "I only remember the good times."

When I told a counselor friend of mine this, she reminded me that it was a mark of how far I had come.

The hurt in my journal entries doesn't exist now, nor does the sadness. Sure, some days it overcomes me, but not in great waves and valleys as it once did. I've worked through it so that I can talk about it without breaking down. Those rough times are gone because I struggled through them. I wrote about them. I thought about them. Some days I still want to talk about Denise and appreciate those who listen. I don't have that need like I once did, but it's another way I choose to honor her because she was a part of my life. It makes me smile to think of her and the fun we had. For the people in my life now who didn't know me when Denise was alive, it's these stories I tell that represent the only way they'll know Denise.

I feel fortunate that I dream about her. Often, we're sitting around the kitchen table as we used to. Or we're very young and playing. When I have these dreams, I'm comforted that Denise is still with me.

On Christmas Eve 1999, it was snowing and I was helping Mom make cookies in the kitchen. Karen and Joe were in the yard playing with the dogs. For just a moment, I felt Denise. I swore I heard her running down the stairs and the swishing of her coat as she made her way to the kitchen, ready to go out and join them in the yard. It was a feeling I've only had once.

Yes, I feel sad she's not here with me as my life moves on, but I know she's looking down on me and helping me continue with my life. No one can ever take our memories away from us. Forgiving the one who died is part of letting go. But you won't forget your sibling by letting him or her go. He or she remains in your heart, just as Denise does in mine.

Take care of yourself and cherish the memories. Work through the difficult times. They become more sporadic if you do. The peaks and valleys eventually subside. The waves mellow out. You'll be okay.

Reflecting on the years since I lost my sister Denise to suicide, I am sometimes baffled at how I survived and got to where I am today. I do know, however, that I worked hard to get here. This book is a testament to my journey so far, as it is one that will continue for the rest of my life.

Once we become sibling survivors of suicide, we are always sibling survivors of suicide. Each time I meet another suicide bereaved, I feel an instant bond to that person. Although we didn't have a choice in joining this group, we make the best of it. Being a suicide bereaved person means we have something to share. We made it through one of the toughest experiences one can have in life. We chose to keep going. And we will continue to not just survive, but to thrive.

By following through on our grief process, our lives will be enriched as never before. We become more aware of others' needs and what we want out of life. We don't want to miss out on more than we already have. We're inspired to mature and become more alert to life around us.

When I am down, I often think of something I heard once: How lucky we are to have someone to whom it was so difficult to say goodbye. We then know we really cared about them.

Michelle Linn-Gust (Rusk), Ph.D.

"A Sister's Message..."

Ball State Daily News
April 2, 1993

Dear Denise:

It was two weeks ago that I came home to cover the men's basketball team in the NCAA Tournament.

I only spent the night before the game at home because Mom and Dad live forty-five minutes from Rosemont Horizon. But I had no idea that when I knocked on your door the morning of the game, to see if you were awake, that it would be the last time I would talk to you.

And to think I couldn't understand what you said to me.

I still can't believe that as I was searching for my seat on press row for the Ball State-Kansas game, you were walking in front of a train—just two weeks before your eighteenth birthday.

I'll never understand why you did what you did. We can only speculate about what was going on in your head. Everyone thought you were getting better, but apparently you thought the bulimia had gotten the best of you and you would never get control of yourself again.

Everything I watched you go through in your high school years was nothing out of the ordinary. It took me to this year to really be happy with myself but I couldn't tell you that because you wouldn't listen.

You were so close to graduation and college—starting all over.

Instead you chose to end your life and leave the mess for the five of us to clean up. I was angry when the high school principal called the weekend after your death to tell us how the school would be open for students needing someone to talk to. A number of the faculty were going into the school on the weekend because of you.

And I watched so many students walk by your casket to pay their last respects. I wonder if you built a wall around yourself and couldn't feel that so many people cared about you. Mom let those who came to the house after the funeral up in your room. They stood in a bunch in the middle of it staring, unsure what to say or do.

Remember Mrs. Martin, the high school journalism adviser? She came to the wake and asked me to stop by the school the next day. The newspaper staff was having a hard time deciding what to print. She thought with my being a journalism major and because you were my sister, I might be able to help them out.

When I got there, I saw how uncomfortable they seemed in talking about your death. Some didn't want to print anything about your death because they knew how unhappy you were at the school.

But that would have been denial that you even died!

You shocked them and everyone else because your smiles and laughter hid so much pain. We knew how you had been depressed for so long and how you tried to kill yourself last fall, but we also thought you had put that behind you.

The night before you died, you were telling me what a great time you had at the spring dance the weekend before.

I'm glad you did get to go to one dance, because there are so many things you'll never get to do, and that bothers me. You only made it halfway up to the 'M' on the mountainside at the University of Montana last summer.

But then, you thought you'd return and have the chance to climb the whole way up. You never got to use the towels I bought you for Christmas to take to college.

Your life was just beginning.

Mom and Dad just wanted to get you out of high school because they knew things would get better after that, but you couldn't do it. When we went to find a cemetery plot for you, I watched them sit in the first pew in the chapel. They are probably hurting more than you could ever imagine.

Instead of four of us kids, there are now three. My name will come after the 'and' in the Christmas cards. I hate that. I don't want to be after the 'and'— that's your spot.

I wanted to come back to school right after the funeral but I felt strange going back to my classes and the newspaper. My life has changed so much and everyone else's is the same. I'll never see you again. Who will trim my hair?

You taught me the game of baseball when I was in high school and now who will go to Kane County Cougars games with me?

I find comfort in the thought that you are out of pain now. I know there is a reason for everything that happens. Your death is no exception, but it bothers me that you had to be everyone else's lesson.

Always, Michelle

Do They Have Bad Days in Heaven?

Afterword

I don't know how long it had been since I read this book last, but I definitely could tell I am in a much different place than that time. I also remember how important it was for me to write it, the passion behind doing it and finding a publisher. I'm grateful that I wrote it when I did as there are events in here I don't remember and the story I would tell today would have different details. It definitely reflects where I was at that time.

I tried only to make changes that didn't reflect the story being told so much as updated language, statistics, and life events (the losses of my parents, the end of a first marriage).

But there is one significant piece that I tried not to change and I decided to address here instead: I am still the same Michelle as before my sister died.

I know, I know, I said I was different and I believed it, but now I see that I am still really her. It feels like I had to travel a road, like a gigantic loop, and much like a running race, you might start in one place, but the finish line might not be in the same exact place, but it's nearby. That's how I feel today.

I see it because I still have the same goals and dreams that I did when Denise was alive– to be a best-selling author, my love for clothes and prints of the 1960s and 1970, the importance of running and swimming pools in my life.

What happened is I took a tour, I had things I had do and I did them. I coped with the loss, I spoke and wrote about it all around the world. I earned more degrees. I did everything I could to help sibling survivors of suicide get the information I knew we all deserved and wasn't available then.

Slowly, I found myself returning to the creativity I had put aside for all of that. The characters in my head kept nagging me to tell their stories, I felt inspired to make clothing and handbags that don't exist like I want it in stores. It was time to hand over the reins and to start Chelle Summer.

In two weeks from the day I write this, Chelle Summer will turn five years old and I'm still in the infancy of what I want to do with it. The inspiration keeps coming. However, I also believe it keeps coming because I found a way to integrate Denise– and my parents– into my life today. They still come to me, they still cheer me on. It's different than it was when they were alive.

But they are definitely still with me. And all their days in heaven are good.

Michelle L. Rusk
July 22, 2020

Do They Have Bad Days in Heaven?

References

Author's note: I didn't update this list because these are the books I used to write this book. There have been many new books published since then and Google searches with reviews are a good resource to find what people have found helpful.

Alexander, Amy and Alvin Poussaint. *Lay My Burden Down: Unraveling Suicide and the Mental Health Crisis Among African Americans.* Boston: Beacon Press, 2000.

Alexander, Victoria. *In the Wake of Suicide: Stories of the People Left Behind.* San Francisco: Jossey-Bass Publishers, 1991.

Alvarez, A. *The Savage God: A Study of Suicide.* New York: W.W. Norton, 1971.

Balk, David E. "Models for Understanding Adolescent Coping with Bereavement." *Death Studies*, 20, 367-387, 1996.

Ball, Aimee Lee. "Why? Trying to Make Sense of Suicide." *Town & Country*, 110-113, 162, May 1996.

Bank, Stephen P. and Michael D. Kahn. *The Sibling Bond.* New York: Basic Books, 1997.

Barrett, Terence. *Life After Suicide: The Survivor's Grief Experience.* Fargo, N.D.: Aftermath Research, 1989.

Batten, Michelle and Kevin Ann Oltjenbruns. "Adolescent Sibling Bereavement as a Catalyst for Spiritual Development: A Model for Understanding." *Death Studies*, 23 (6), 529, 546, 1999.

Before Their Time: Memorial Songs and Music, Vol. I. Hospice of Vermont/New Hampshire, 1999. (Three volumes are now available.) (February 23, 2001).

Bloom, Lois. *Mourning, After Suicide.* Cleveland: The Pilgrim Press, 1986.

Bolton, Iris. *My Son...My Son...A Guide to Healing After Death, Loss, or Suicide.* Atlanta: Bolton Press, 1983.

Brent, David A., and others. "The Impact of Adolescent Suicide on Siblings and Parents: A Longitudinal Follow-Up." *Suicide and Life-Threatening Behavior*, 26 (3), 253-259, Fall 1996.

Brent, David A., and others. "Psychiatric Impact of the Loss of an Adolescent Sibling to Suicide." *Journal of Affective Disorders*, 28, 249-256, 1993.

Calhoun, Lawrence G. and Breon G. Allen. "Social Reactions to the Survivor of Suicide in the Family: A Review of the Literature." *Omega*, 23 (2), 95-107, 1991.

Carlson, Trudy. *Suicide Survivors' Handbook: A Guide for the Bereaved and Those Who Wish to Help Them.* Duluth, Minn.: Benline Press, 1995.

Catechism of the Catholic Church. Mahwah, N.J.: Paulist Press, 1994.

Cerel, J., Brown, M., Maple, M., Singleton, M., van de Venne, J, Moore, M. & Flaherty, C (2018). How many people are exposed to suicide? Not six. *Suicide and Life Threatening Behavior* https://doi.org/10.1111/sltb.12450

Cicirelli, Victor G. *Sibling Relationships Across the Life Span.* New York: Plenum, 1995.

Colgrove, Melba, Harold Bloomfield, and Peter McWilliams. *How to Survive the Loss of a Love.* Los Angeles: Prelude Press, 1991.

Colt, George Howe. *The Enigma of Suicide.* New York: Summit Books, 1991.

Conndis, Ingrid A. "Life Transitions and the Adult Sibling Tie: A Qualitative Study." *Journal of Marriage and Family*, 54, 972-982, November 1992.

Conndis, Ingrid A. "Siblings as Friends in Later Life." *A merican Behavioral Scientist*, 33 (1), 81-93, 1989.

Crenshaw, David A. *Bereavement: Counseling the Grieving Throughout the Life Cycle.* New York: Crossroad, 1990.

Davies, Betty. *Shadows in the Sun: The Experience of Sibling Bereavement in Childhood.* Philadelphia: Taylor & Francis, 1999.

Demi, Alice Sterner and Carol Howell. "Hiding and Healing: Resolving the Suicide of a Parent or Sibling." *Archives of* DeSpelder, Lynne Ann and Albert Lee Strickland. *The Last Dance.* Mt. View, Calif.: Mayfield, 1992.

Derrek, Kirsten. *Dancing with the Skeleton: Meditations for Suicide Survivors.* Omaha: Centering Corporation, 1995.

Doka, Kenneth J. (ed.). *Living with Grief After Sudden Loss.* Bristol, Pa.: Taylor & Francis, 1996.

Donnelly, Katherine Fair. *Recovering from the Loss of a Sibling.* New York: Dodd, Mead & Company, 1988.

Dorland's Illustrated Medical Dictionary. Philadelphia: W. B. Saunders, 1981.

Dunn, Judy. *Sisters and Brothers: The Developing Child.* Cambridge, Mass.: Harvard University Press, 1985.

Dunne, Edward J., John L. McIntosh, and Karen Dunne-Maxim (eds.). *Suicide and Its Aftermath: Understanding and Counseling the Survivors.* New York: W.W. Norton, 1987.

Dunne-Maxim, Karen. "A Sister's Story." *Lifesavers*, 7 (4), 8, Fall 1995.

Eyetsemitan, Frank. "Stifled Grief in the Workplace." *Death Studies*, 22 (5), 469-479, 1998.

Farrant, Ann. *Sibling Bereavement: Helping Children Cope with Loss.* Herndon, Va.: Cassell, 1998.

Fine, Carla. *No Time to Say Goodbye: Surviving the Suicide of a Loved One.* New York: Doubleday, 1997.

Finneran, Kathleen. *The Tender Land: A Family Love Story.* New York: Houghton Mifflin, 2000.

Fitzgerald, Helen. *The Mourning Handbook.* New York: Fireside, 1994.

Gliko-Braden, Majel. *Grief Comes to Class: An Educator's Guide.* Omaha: Centering Corporation, 1992.

Glover, Beryl S. *The Empty Chair: The Journey of Grief After Suicide.* Oklahoma City: In-Sight Books, 2000.

Grollman, Earl A. *Suicide: Prevention, Intervention, Postvention.* Boston: Beacon Press, 1988.

Grollman, Earl A. and Max Malikow. *Living When a Young Friend Commits Suicide.* Boston: Beacon Press, 1999.

Hewett, John H. *After Suicide.* Philadelphia: Westminster Press, 1980.

Hogan, Nancy S. and Daryl B. Greenfield. "Adolescent Sibling Bereavement Symptomatology in a Large Community Sample." *Journal of Adolescent Research*, 6 (1), 97-112, 1991.

Irwin, Cait. *Conquering the Beast Within: How I Fought Depression and Won...And How You Can, Too.* New York: Times Books, 1998.

James, John W. and Frank Cherry. *The Grief Recovery Handbook: A Step-by-Step Program for Moving Beyond Loss.* New York: Harper Perennial, 1988.

Jamison, Kay Redfield. *An Unquiet Mind: A Memoir of Moods and Madness.* New York: Vintage Books, 1995.

Jamison, Kay Redfield. *Night Falls Fast: Understanding Suicide.* New York: Vintage Books, 1999.

Kelly, Lynn. *Don't Ask for the Dead Man's Golf Clubs: Advice for Friends When Someone Dies.* Littleton, Colo.: Kelly Communications, 2000.

Kosterlitz, Melissa Irvine. "A Survivor's Story: Melissa Irvine Kosterlitz." *Lifesavers*, 5 (3), 6-7, Summer 1993.

Krysinski, Patricia Rosenkranz. "Coping with Suicide: Beyond the Five-Day Bereavement Leave Policy." *Death Studies*, 17, 173-177, 1993.

Kuklin, Susan. *After a Suicide: Young People Speak Up.* New York: G. P. Putnam's Sons, 1994.

Leenaars, Antoon A. and Susanne Wenckstern. "Principles of Postvention: Applications to Suicide and Trauma in Schools." *Death Studies*, 22 (4), 357-391, 1998.

Lukas, Christopher and Henry M. Seiden. *Silent Grief:*
Living in the Wake of Suicide. Northvale, N.J.: Jason Aronson, 1997.

Marcus, Eric. *Why Suicide?* San Francisco: Harper Collins, 1996.

McIntosh, John L. "Survivors of Suicide: A Comprehensive Bibliography
Update, 1986-1995." *Omega*, 33 (2), 147-175,1996.

McIntosh, John L. (2019). *U.S.A. Suicide: 2018 Official Final Data.*
http://pages.iu.edu/~jmcintos/SuicideDataCompiled.htm. (July 15, 2020).

Merrell, Susan Scarf. *The Accidental Bond: The Power of Sibling*
Relationships. New York: Times Books, 1995.

Miller, Sara Swan. *An Empty Chair: Living in the Wake of a Sibling's Suicide.*
New York: Writer's Club Press, 2000.

National Institute of Mental Health. *Suicide Facts*, 1997.
www.nimh.nih.gov. (February 21, 2001).

Nelson, Richard E. and Judith C. Galas. *The Power to Prevent Suicide:*
A Guide for Teens Helping Teens.
Minneapolis: Free Spirit Publishing, 1994.

Osterweis, Marian, Fredric Solomon, and Morris Green (eds.).
Bereavement: Reactions, Consequences, and Care.
Washington, D.C.: National Academy Press, 1984.

Rando, Therese. *Grieving: How to Go on Living When Someone You Love*
Dies. Lexington, Mass.: Lexington Books, 1988.

Range, Lillian M. and William C. Goggin. "Reactions to Suicide: Does Age of
the Victim Make a Difference?" *Death Studies*, 14, 269-275, 1990.

Raphael, Beverley. *Anatomy of Bereavement.*
New York: Basic Books, 1983.

Riches, Gordon and Pam Dawson. *An Intimate Loneliness: Supporting*
Bereaved Parents and Siblings. Philadelphia:
Open University Press, 2000.

Robinson, Rita. *Survivors of Suicide.* Van Nuys, Calif.:
Newcastle Publishing, 1989.

Rosen, Helen. *Unspoken Grief: Coping with Childhood Sibling Loss.* Lexington, Mass.: Lexington Books, 1986.

Rosenfield, Linda and Marilynne Prupas. *Left Alive: After a Suicide Death in the Family.* Springfield, Ill.: Charles C. Thomas, 1994.

Rosof, Barbara D. *The Worst Loss: How Families Heal from the Death of a Child.* New York: Holt, 1994.

Ross, E. Betsy. *Life After Suicide: A Ray of Hope for Those Left Behind.* New York: Insight Books, 1997.

Sanders, Catherine M. *Surviving Grief...And Learning to Live Again.* New York: John Wiley & Sons, 1992.

Sanderson, Kim. "Wish You Were Here..." *Zoot Capri*, 22-25 Fall/Winter 1992.

Scrivani, Mark. *When Death Walks In.* Omaha: Centering Corporation, 1991.

Shneidman, Edwin S. (ed.) *On the Nature of Suicide.* San Francisco: Jossey-Bass Publishers, 1969.

Silence of the Heart, produced by James O'Fallon and directed by Richard Michaels, EDDE Entertainment, 1993 (1984), television movie.

Smolin, Ann and John Guinan. *Healing After the Suicide of a Loved One.* New York: Fireside, 1993.

Stimming, Mary and Maureen Stimming (eds.). *Before Their Time: Adult Children's Experiences of Parental Suicide.* Philadelphia: Temple University, 1999.

Stroebe, Margaret S., Wolfgang Stroebe, and Robert O. Hansson (eds.). *Handbook of Bereavement.* Cambridge, Mass.: University Press, 1993.

Stuadacher, Carol. *Beyond Grief: A Guide for Recovering from the Death of a Loved One.* Oakland, Calif.: New Harbinger Publications, 1987.

Staudacher, Carol. *Men & Grief.* Oakland, Calif.: New Harbinger Publications, 1991.

Tatelbaum, Judy. *The Courage to Grieve: Creative Living, Recovery, and Growth Through Grief.* New York: Harper & Row, 1980.

Traisman, Enid Samuel. *I Remember, I Remember: A Keepsake Journal.* Omaha: Centering Corporation, 1994.

U.S. Census Bureau. *Table 1, Families by Type, Age, Metropolitan-Nonmetropolitan Residence, and Race and Hispanic Origin of the Householder: March 1998*

www.census.gov/population/www/socdemo/hhfam.html. (February 20, 2001).

U.S. Public Health Service. *The Surgeon General's Call to Action to Prevent Suicide.* Washington, D.C., 1999. www.surgeongeneral.gov. (February 21, 2001).

Van Dongen, Carol J. "The Legacy of Suicide." *Journal of Psychosocial Nursing,* 26 (1), 9-13, 1988.

Van Dongen, Carol J. "Social Context of Postsuicide Bereavement." *Death Studies,* 17, 125-141, 1993.

Wechsler, James A. *In a Darkness: A Story of Young Suicide.* Miami: The Pickering Press, 1988.

Wolfelt, Alan D. *Healing Your Grieving Heart: 100 Practical Ideas.* Fort Collins, Colo.: Companion Press, 1998.

Wolfelt, Alan D. *Healing the Grieving Heart: 100 Practical Ideas for Families, Friends & Caregivers.* Fort Collins, Colo.: Companion Press, 1998.

Wrobleski, Adina. *Suicide: Why?* Minneapolis: Afterwords, 1989.

For Children

Blackburn, Lynn Bennett. *I Know I Made It Happen: A Gentle Book About Feelings.* Omaha: Centering Corporation, 1991.

Goldman, Linda. *Bart Speaks Out: Breaking the Silence on Suicide.* Los Angeles: Western Psychological Services, 1998.

Heegaard, Marge. *When Something Terrible Happens: Children Can Learn to Cope with Grief.* Minneapolis: Woodland Press, 1991.

O'Toole, Donna and Jerre Cory. *Helping Children Grieve and Grow.* Burnsville, N.C.: Compassion Press, 1998.

Rogers, Fred. *So Much to Think About: When Someone You Care About Has Died.* Pittsburgh: Family Communications, 1991.

Rubel, Barbara. *But I Didn't Say Goodbye: For Parents and Professionals Helping Child Suicide Survivors.* Kendall Park, N.J.: Griefwork Center, 1999.

Traisman, Enid Samuel. *A Child Remembers: A Write-in Memory Book for Bereaved Children.* Omaha: Centering Corporation, 1994.

Winsch, Jane Loretta. *After the Funeral.* New York: Paulist Press, 1995.

Wolfelt, Alan D. *Healing Your Grieving Heart: 100 Practical Ideas for Kids.* Fort Collins, Colo.: Companion Press, 2000.

Wolfelt, Alan D. *Healing the Grieving Child's Heart: 100 Practical Ideas for Families, Friends & Caregivers.* Fort Collins, Colo.: Companion Press, 2000.

For Adolescents

Traisman, Enid Samuel. *Fire in My Heart, Ice in My Veins: A Journal for Teenagers Experiencing a Loss.* Omaha: Centering Corporation, 1992.

Wolfelt, Alan D. *Healing Your Grieving Heart for Teens: 100 Practical Ideas.* Fort Collins, Colo.: Companion Press, 1998.

Wolfelt, Alan D. *Healing a Teen's Grieving Heart: 100 Practical Ideas for Families, Friends & Caregivers.* Fort Collins, Colo.: Companion Press, 2001.

Resources

The following organizations offer information and services for the suicide bereaved. While there are many organizations available, we recommend starting with these two:

American Association of Suicidology

5221 Wisconsin Avenue, NW, 2nd Floor

Washington, D.C. 20015

202-237-2280

www.suicidology.org

American Foundation for Suicide Prevention

199 Water Street, 11th Floor

New York, NY 10038

212-363-3500

www.afsp.org

Also by Michelle Linn-Gust:

Ginger's Gift: Hope and Healing through Dog Companionship

Rocky Roads: The Journeys of Families through Suicide Grief

A Winding Road: A Handbook for those Supporting the Suicide Bereaved
(edited with John Peters)

Seeking Hope: Stories of the Suicide Bereaved (edited with Julie Cerel)

Sisters: The Karma Twist

The Australian Pen Pal

As Michelle. L. Rusk:

The Green Dress

Flowers by Day, Stars by Night: Finding Happiness after Loss and Change

That Cooking Girl